Fiery

A daily companion for challenging times

You are being called to love against all odds, regardless of your circumstances, regardless of how others may treat you. That is the nature of Love, Fiery Love.

Also by Moyra Irving:

Take Me to the Mountain – discovering the you that never dies

Published by Inspirational Storytellers 2013

INSPIRATIONAL STORYTELLERS

First published in 2015 by Inspirational Storytellers

Design: Tony & Lesley Bailey
Layout: John Beaumont
Cover Art: *Fiery Love,* a painting by Moyra Irving

For Maz -
the bravest woman I know

Acknowledgments

As we grow older we come to realise how very little we know. Nevertheless, I thank all who have encouraged me to share what I have learned, and am still learning, and to write this second book, a sequel to *Take Me to the Mountain – discovering the you that never dies.*

My thanks again to Nancy Seifer for agreeing to read my manuscript before it was complete, and to Cecilia St. King for doing so despite her busy schedule touring America as a Peace Troubadour. Your enthusiasm and wonderful reviews leave me honoured beyond words. Gratitude also to Stephen Kalinich, the celebrated American poet, spoken word artist and *Beach Boys* lyricist, for allowing me to share his lines: *The greatest way to success* (Chapter 5).

Contents

Foreword

***Fiery Love* is a balm. It gifts the reader with a deep breath. Like reading Moyra Irving's first book, *Take Me to the Mountain*, it is like sitting down with a good, wise friend who helps you to remember your soul's purpose and why we are all here on this earth. The remarkable thing is, that friend turns out to be you. *Fiery Love* takes you home to 'you.'**

Cecilia St King

Cecilia St. King is a charismatic Peace Troubadour who performs original songs with positive spiritual messages. Translating her esoteric studies of The Ageless Wisdom Teachings into song, her concerts offer a powerful antidote to turmoil in our current times. Cecilia is no stranger to adversity. Six months after running from the fall of The World Trade Center, she was diagnosed with cancer in her throat. She spent time healing in a monastery in New Zealand and turned her tragedy into triumph by being a voice for Peace.

www.ceciliastking.com Endorsed by the M.K. Gandhi Institute for Nonviolence.

When Moyra Irving writes about love, she speaks with the voice of one who *knows* the essence of spiritual love from deep experience. I found this to be true in *Take Me to the Mountain* as I do in her new book, *Fiery Love.* It is the love of the soul that heals, and the purpose of *Fiery Love* is to bring the reader in touch with this healing force lying within each one of us.

Nancy Seifer

Nancy Seifer was a social and political activist before finding her way to the spiritual path. In the 1960s she was a Peace Corps volunteer in West Africa, a staff member at the African-American Institute in New York City, and an aide for ethnic affairs to New York City Mayor, John V. Lindsay. In the 70s she directed a program on women and diversity at the Institute on American Pluralism. While there she wrote papers, monographs, and chapters for anthologies on working-class women, and later a book (*Nobody Speaks for Me!*, 1976, Simon & Schuster) still in use at colleges and universities. Her articles appeared in *The New York Times*, *The Village Voice*, and *Ms. Magazine*.

Nancy is co-author of *When the Soul Awakens:*

The Path to Spiritual Evolution and a New World Era

www.whenthesoulawakens.org

Part 1
An Introduction to Retreat

Introduction

This is a very simple book. It is written for anyone who suffers, as we all do at times, in the hope it will bring you – the reader – the gift of solace, companionship, and above all, Love.

Fiery Love offers a new perspective for daily living, one that relies entirely on self-compassion, presence, and rest. It is also a down-to-earth guide to the *other-worldly* and to this end I have been careful to strip it of as much spiritual jargon as I can. Overtly 'spiritual' language can often alienate and confuse, so my intention is just this: to *point you to yourself*, to that part of you that already 'knows' far more than you imagine.

Retreat is the journey to this seat of knowing: that aspect of us that is beyond suffering, even beyond death - the eternal Self.

Without drawing on any specific belief systems I will refer occasionally to an ancient body of knowledge known as *The Ageless Wisdom* teachings. This will, I hope, spark interest in anyone who ponders the deeper meaning of Life. *Ageless Wisdom* lies behind all major religions and spiritual philosophies and is concerned with the

evolution of consciousness, and our place and purpose within creation.
Any autobiographical details are included purely to illustrate various themes.

The Nature of Love

Fiery Love is the eternal flame within every heart, also known as the Christ Principle. What distinguishes it from ordinary mortal love is its impartiality. It is what we all seek yet find so elusive, yet it is at the same time the very thing that underlies our whole existence. It is what makes us both human and divine.
Love in the truest sense is a state of being rather than an emotion; a magnetic force that binds together everything and everyone in creation; a love therefore that is not dependent on perceived worth or personal preference.

The Nature of Fire

Metaphorically, Fire (or Light) has many qualities. Throughout our retreat we shall call upon these fiery qualities to nourish and inspire us each day:

- Fire is creative - the very Fire that brought us into being.[1] It inspires in us passion, confidence, purpose, and meaning
- Fire illuminates our view of ourselves and the world around us. (In the Buddha's teachings,

light is the symbol of truth that dispels the darkness of ignorance)

- Fire purges and transforms - it helps to destroy our illusions and re-shape us into better versions of our selves
- Fire is an expression of Love - it warms, comforts, and heals. It too gives purpose and meaning to our lives

Love, the Great Healer

Our Inner Fire possesses all of these qualities but the greatest of these is Love. Self-love, self-understanding, and self-compassion are the foundations of a loving nature and only when we feel deep compassion for ourselves can we express this meaningfully to others.

Retreat enables us to enter into the deepest possible relationship with ourselves; to *understand* and accept all that we are, and all that we have been. Understanding restores peace of mind and soothes our own pain. It lies at the heart of forgiveness and leads potentially to reconciliation (the 'binding together again' of that which is broken).

Retreat – coming home to your Self

Fiery Love makes personal retreat accessible to all. It caters especially for those who haven't the resources to travel to some distant utopia, free from the pressures of daily living. Instead, it allows you to gently penetrate the heart of your daily challenges, while at the same time enjoying the benefits of refuge. Retreat brings you home to your Self.

Resting, Noticing, Self-compassion

Throughout your retreat you will be developing three vital *attitudes:*

- *Resting (learning how to relax, even while you work)*
- *Noticing (becoming aware, moment-to-moment, of the Eternal Now)*
- *Self-compassion*

These three 'attitudes' are reinforced through five Pathways (*The Wordless Way, Awareness, Healing & Transformation, Blessing,* and *Fiery Love).* There are also forty new Daily Messages with commentaries on each one. Being somewhat cautious about 'channelled' messages, I make no claims as to their authorship though this is not to diminish their value. Far from it; for me the Messages have been, and always are, a Blessing. I ask only that you reflect on them and take from them whatever you find helpful.

To their source I offer my gratitude for its Guiding Light. My own life has been inspired by it and my hope is that yours will be too.

Each Message deepens our sense of love, compassion and understanding - qualities that enhance our own well-being and ultimately enable us to reach out to others

Mini Retreats

If you are not able to do the full 40 days in one go you may like to try a series of 8 day mini-retreats instead, beginning with **The Wordless Way (Chapter Three)**. The other Pathways will then form the basis of future retreats whenever you choose. *Fiery Love* can be enjoyed again and again. Indeed, it is strongly recommended that you repeat your retreat at frequent intervals. Each time will be different – because you will be too.

Coming Home: the Human Journey

In *Take Me to the Mountain,* I used the mountain (or upward pointing triangle) as a symbol of human aspiration and ascent. Ascent is our natural inclination to reach for something beyond ourselves; to test and transcend the limits of our endurance. In *Fiery Love* we explore its sister pathway: descent (the reversed triangle or downward path).

Of course, these two pathways are not really separate at all. We make the two journeys simultaneously – the upward and downward - a paradox that allows us to reach our highest potential while plumbing the depths of our personal circumstances. They both lead us home.

Indeed, it is precisely through our daily tests and trials that we grow in self-awareness and understanding. Yes, it's right down here in the thick of things that we 'ascend,' and ultimately transcend our difficulties. It is here too, when we open our hearts to patience and self-compassion, that we discover our Inner Companion and the deeper meaning of Love: *Fiery Love.*

May you be well, may you be happy, may you be free from suffering [2]

1 According to the Ageless Wisdom teachings: *Cosmic fire forms the background of our evolution* (*Letters on Occult Meditation,* Alice A. Bailey, Lucis Trust Publishing). That is to say 'The One Life' (the One in Whom we live and move and have our being) manifests through all forms within the universe as fiery energy. (*A Treatise on Cosmic Fire*)

2 May you be well, may you be happy, may you be free from suffering
Metta Bhavana is a Buddhist practice, intended to develop loving kindness. *Mettā* or *maitrī* cultivates benevolence to all living beings. The practice begins with an attitude of loving kindness to oneself. It next focuses, equally and in turn, on a good friend, a 'neutral' person, a difficult person, and then gradually embraces the entire universe.

Chapter One
Before You Begin

This chapter shows you how to plan your retreat in advance.
I have incorporated various self-care tips, such as preparing healthy meals, creating time for leisure activities, and being kind to yourself, along with ideas for managing your daily routine (especially if you are working or caring for others). My hope is that by the end of your retreat you will have enjoyed a pleasant and life-changing experience.

Since *Fiery Love* is intended for those who are challenged and maybe suffering pain, loneliness and loss, the emphasis is on comfort and companionship. It is not designed to overwhelm you with exercises but instead to make each day more relaxing, creative and purposeful.

Managing pain[1]
Many hospital pain clinics now recognise the benefits of relaxation and mindfulness since both

of these practices have been found to boost the body's immunity and natural pain modifiers. Resistance and control create tension which in turn increases discomfort. 'Noticing' (being mindful) can help us to face and accept things as they are, rather than how we want them to be.

Although this does not imply that we should resign ourselves to pain, *relaxing* and *noticing* are tools that potentially free us from our emotional battle with suffering, and in this sense can be very empowering. The same is true for non-physical pain. Anxiety and depression, feelings of guilt, unworthiness, anger, bereavement, and loneliness can all be eased by an initial acceptance of their existence, followed by relaxation techniques, and a loosening of control.

Whenever we're in pain – whether physical or emotional – the mind tends to seize upon memories of other painful events. This happens so quickly that we may well be unaware of them. But such thoughts ('secondary suffering'), combined with our current pain, can escalate into enormous anxiety and feelings of despair. Fear and tension then create more fear ... and more pain still. As a result the brain becomes increasingly alert to discomfort. (Brain scans even show that chronic pain sufferers have substantially more brain tissue assigned to it.)

Yet there is hope. It appears also that mindfulness practices can actually change our brain patterns. These then affect the brain structure so that over time our experience of pain becomes less intense.

Fiery Love and the Legacy of Pain

Pain is part of our earthly experience, something we all have to suffer from time to time.

However, we are also miraculously enabled to bear adversity, and in some cases even flourish as a result.

Human beings endure the most intolerable pain and loss yet many still manage to live rich and meaningful lives. For some the legacy of pain is bitterness and resentment, but for others it becomes understanding, empathy and compassion. Pain teaches us to 'feel with' others in their own suffering. At such times we witness Fiery Love and the triumph of the human spirit. **(See Chapter Five: Helping Others is Good for You)**

Through suffering we learn that it isn't what happens to us that matters but how we deal with it. *Our task then is to learn - through lifetimes of trial and error - how to adapt to hardship, and how to view life differently.* This is a vital part of our evolutionary journey.

Dealing with Grief and Loss

Grief is a natural but painful response to the loss of anyone or anything significant in our lives, such as:

- death of a close family member, partner or pet
- divorce or ending of a friendship
- loss of a job; redundancy or retirement
- loss of part of ourselves, loss of health, a serious operation
- moving home
- children leaving home
- the ageing process - approaching adolescence, middle age and old age can all involve feelings of loss of identity and sadness

Change is an inevitable part of life and something most of us wish to avoid. Even positive life changes involve loss. Loss of identity (such as getting married, becoming a parent, or retiring) can trigger feelings of sadness and mourning for the 'old self,' or way of life.

Loss reminds us of own mortality and the impermanence of physical life.

Grieving is as individual as we are. It may result in panic attacks and physical symptoms such as weight change, tiredness, insomnia or unexplained pain and discomfort.
It is a process that takes an unspecified time and requires a good deal of patience, compassion, and self-care. Given such conditions grief will heal naturally and in its own time.
Symptoms of grief may arise on and off – these can include overwhelming feelings of shock, numbness and disbelief, deep sadness, loneliness, and powerlessness. There may be anger and resentment too ('Why is this happening to me?'), or self-blame and regret ('It's my fault, I should have done more').

At such times it's important to express your feelings and turn to others for support; to family and friends and anyone who can share your sorrow. You might also consider bereavement counselling to help you to work through your emotions.
If you have a religious belief or spiritual path you may well find solace here. Conversely if you have

lost all connection with your faith (maybe as a result of your loss), consider asking others to pray on your behalf or offer healing. **(See also Chapter Six: Blessing)**

The stress involved in grieving means that you now need to take extra care of yourself. Entering daily retreat is a good way to begin.

Finding Time for Yourself

For many people 'spare' time is a luxury. However, it's not how much time you have that counts but *how* you spend it. Making time for 'you' is vital – especially if you are caring for others and living with the added stress of pain, loneliness or loss.

Finding time for your self is an act of kindness to you and to others. When you are less stressed you will be a much easier person to be around.

Loneliness – becoming your own companion

Your daily appointment with yourself is equally important whether you live alone or with others. Loneliness is a feeling of separation and can exist even if you have friends and family around you. The stilling techniques suggested in *Fiery Love* can help you release the fear of loneliness and become your own good companion.

You might also consider joining a group to pursue a personal interest (local history, arts and crafts, a foreign language, creative writing, photography, rambling, and so on) – or even try volunteering. While research shows that social isolation is a major health risk factor, it also suggests that people who do volunteer work are much less likely to suffer illness. Lots of charitable organisations are keen to recruit helpers and this too can be a very worthwhile and enjoyable way to meet others and build self-esteem.[2]

Planning ahead

Being on retreat while living in the world is remarkably simple.. *Fiery Love* is designed to make your life *easier* by using your usual everyday activities as material for retreat. Here are 11 ways to get the most out of your retreat:

1. Read the book

I suggest you read this book in its entirety before you 'arrive' on retreat (**Chapter Three**). This way you will know exactly what it has in store for you. I also recommend you allow 2 days of 'easing in' prior to beginning your retreat. This will give you a chance to practise those three vital attitudes: *resting, noticing, and most of all, self-love.*

2. Book your retreat

Make a formal appointment with yourself and enter your intended retreat dates and times in your diary. This way you are more likely to take it seriously and see it through to the end.

3. Plan your shopping in advance for simple, fresh and nutritious food for a week at a time.

Your retreat is a perfect opportunity to take extra care of yourself. There is no universally perfect diet so choose one best suited to your own needs. Simple, nutritious food will give your digestion and immune system a boost. Include fresh foods (preferably organic and vegetarian). Eat plenty of fresh fruit, salads and vegetables to increase alkalinity, along with whole grains and pulses. Eat things you like and avoid those you don't - eating should be pleasurable. Having said that, avoid all processed foods and especially refined sugar, and limit dairy products as far as possible. Homemade soups are excellent and very easy to prepare. Above all your food and its preparation should be enjoyable!

4. Have access to filtered water, the purest you can find. You will need to drink 7-8 glasses of water (hot or cold) each day. Herbal, fruit, or green teas are excellent but coffee is best avoided (although substitutes made with chicory or barley can be used).

For a healthy chocolate treat (especially during the autumn and winter months) warm coconut milk with cacao or cocoa powder makes a delicious bedtime drink!

Half a teaspoonful of sodium bicarbonate, taken morning and evening in warm water, is a traditional health tonic that increases alkalinity.

5. Bedtime

Retreat is an opportunity to go to bed a little earlier than usual. Adequate sleep and a regular lifestyle are essential for health and may even be implicated in longevity. [3]

Treat yourself to a massage whenever you can. Have ready some essential oils for bathing or a lotion for self-massage after bathing or showering. (I find lavender, frankincense and rose beneficial but you may have your own special favourites.)

Before retiring, prepare a flask of hot water for your waking drink. Add a slice of lemon, lime or some herbal/fruit tea if preferred.

6. Keep a journal or notebook to hand for your morning and evening 'silent sitting' times.

7. Shh! I'm on retreat!

There is no need for anyone else to know you are on retreat – apart from those you live with of course. Your daily routine requires 20-30 minutes in the morning and evening when you will be unavailable.

These will be your 'silent sitting' times so you may need to negotiate with those involved. It's a good idea to limit phone calls and internet use (strongly advised at this time!), but otherwise your retreat will go unnoticed – from the outside at least.

Remember - retreat means to 'draw back.' Be flexible and resourceful. If quiet time is not feasible because of young children or other dependents, plan your silent sitting for a more suitable time of day. (You might use your lunch break at work or even sit in your car for those silent moments).

Invest in good ear plugs for your 'silent sittings' if noise is a problem. (I find silicone earplugs the most effective.)

8. Develop an 'attitude of retreat' in advance:
Restfulness, noticing, and self-compassion are three 'attitudes of retreat' that will serve you for the rest of your life:

(a) Restfulness: this is all my time anyway!
Treat this time as a holiday, a real opportunity for rest. It is to be enjoyed so why not make the most of it!
Remember that 'all time is your own,' no matter what the demands. Therefore, the next time you feel frustrated or bored try telling yourself: 'Actually, this is still my own time.' This may well change how you feel about your work, household chores, or even having to spend time with people you'd rather avoid. It's all your own time! Remember to *relax while you're working and relax while you're resting* - this may sound obvious but it's all part of developing an attitude of retreat while living and working in the world.

(b) Noticing
Noticing enables us to view life at a little distance. This helps us to deal with the ups and

downs of life without being overwhelmed by them. It's a way of observing, accepting, and understanding our feelings without suppressing them.

Practise with the little things, everyday situations and encounters, until noticing becomes second-nature. When we watch our life from a distance we recognise those familiar thoughts and fears (the 'what if's') that disturb our peace of mind.
Most of us have learned to look for happiness in the world outside yet in the end true contentment can only arise from within. Retreat reinforces our sense of fulfilment and self-love.

(c) Self-compassion
Learn to love yourself. Be kind! Notice when you are being less than kind to yourself; when you expect too much of yourself; when you forget to listen to your own needs.
Try leaving yourself little reminders - to 'rest,' 'notice,' and 'be kind.' Stick 'Post-It' notes on your bathroom mirror, in the kitchen, on your bedside table, in the car.

9. Raising your Spirits
Don't forget to find a little time for leisure activities:

(a) Exercise

Movement increases physical, mental and emotional circulation. It raises the spirits and releases tension caused by worry, anger, irritation, grief and so on.

Choose an activity that you really enjoy:
Walking, swimming, cycling, dancing, yoga, Qi Gong, Tai Chi, and time at the gym are all great forms of exercise. Maybe try something different, or join a class where you will meet new people. Walking is especially good as it can stimulate creative thought. It also allows for time spent in Nature. A few minutes spent each day, 'touching the earth,' is deeply healing. Half an hour spent outside (in the garden, a local park or countryside), surrounded by the wonders of creation, deepens our appreciation of the world we live in.

If you are bed-ridden you may be able to try simple forms of exercise such as stretching and Hand Yoga[4]

(b) Creativity

Creative self-expression is excellent therapy and can be deeply comforting. It gives us purpose and a new perspective on our life. Through

writing especially we get to view ourselves at a distance; and when we see our life on the page we also gain understanding – of the things that have happened to us and the choices we have made. We then realise how much we have learned from our experiences. Writing is known to be good for the health and also stimulates the memory.
You may find that unexpected words come to you in the form of stories, poems, letters or even guidance of some kind. Just relax and allow the inspiration to come.

There are many ways to be creative. You don't have to be a skilled artist, photographer, musician or writer either: you can express your creativity in the most elementary and simple ways. You might experiment with new recipes, decorate a room or plant flowers in the garden. **Again, whatever you do, enjoy it!**

10. Your Daily Routine

Each retreat day will begin with your **20 minute Morning Practice**. Be flexible and always adapt your retreat to suit your circumstances.

(a) If you share a bedroom you may need to use somewhere else for your practice. Ideally it begins with a 5 minute period of **Silent Sitting** as soon as you are awake. Silent Sitting involves gentle, conscious breathing: *breathing in and knowing you are breathing in; breathing out and knowing you are breathing out.*

(b) You will then be ready to rest in your 'High Place.' This is an energy centre between the eyebrows, the *Ajna* or brow centre, a place where you focus your attention and gently observe yourself.

(c) Then follows your Message for the day (10-15 minutes).
This will include your **Morning Resolve,** an intention you set for the day (e.g. a decision to relax, be aware, be kind or patient, etc.)

(d) You can use any remaining time to record your thoughts or insights in your notebook or journal.

(e) The rest of your day until the **Evening Review** will be spent **relaxing** (yes, even if you are at work!), **noticing, and practising self-compassion.** Apart from lunch, do try to have a short morning and afternoon break (even 5 minutes is enough). This will give you an opportunity for more silent sitting and conscious breathing, and time to rest in your 'High Place.'

(f) Evening Practice: In the Tibetan Buddhist tradition there is a certain preparation for death called the *Life Review*. This is intended to help the dying person make their journey out of the body, free of any unresolved thoughts and feelings. It is a time to face yourself, honestly and sincerely, and to make peace. During your **Evening Review** look back on your day as objectively as you can. Notice 'how you have been' and the choices you have made. Remain relaxed, compassionate and non-judgmental.

The Evening Review is a great opportunity to clear the mind before the journey into sleep. This winding-down period will also include time for your journal and reading (anything conducive to sleep and not over-stimulating).

11. The Evening Before

The evening before your retreat, find a few moments to sit quietly.

Ask yourself why you have decided to enter retreat and what you hope to gain from it. Make notes in your journal for future

reference. You will need to look at these again at the end of your retreat.
Notice how it feels to spend this time in silence without any distractions. The world we live in is a busy place; we communicate more than ever before, often to excess via mobile phones and the internet. Children especially are over-stimulated as a result of television and electronic games and have little time to develop their sense of 'Self'. Likewise where programmes of formal learning begin at a very early age (as early as 4 or 5 in some countries) children have less opportunity to explore their Inner Life.[5]

Silence, our first Pathway to retreat, deepens our awareness of the Life within Form, the Eternal Self. This exists whether we have a body or not which means we need never be afraid to die.

The purpose of retreat is to help you to identify with this Eternal Self. When you do it will change your life for ever.

1 For further details see: *Mindfulness: A Practical Guide to Relieving Pain, Reducing Stress and Restoring Wellbeing* by Vidyamala Burch and Dr Danny Penman (Piatkus). This book won the BMA's Best Book (Popular Medicine) Award 2014.

2 *The Extra Guest* is an end-hunger charity which is run entirely by volunteers. If you are interested in helping us please contact co-founder Moyra Irving:
moyrairving@yahoo.co.uk www.theextraguest.com

3 According to many ancient traditions, the potential life span of the human body is 120 years. To achieve longevity it is important to live in harmony with the natural rhythms of your body, the soul's vehicle of expression. When your body is healthy, your soul is able to fulfil its highest potential.

4 *Mudras: Yoga in your hands* by Gertrud Hirschi (Weiser 2000)

5 Evidence suggests that early formal education may damage a child's wellbeing and longer-term levels of attainment. The Save Childhood Movement's campaign *Too Much, Too Soon* was created in response to increasing concerns around this issue.
It maintains that the longer young children can spend in playful and creatively focussed environments, the more likely they are to develop happily and healthily.

Chapter Two
Coming Home

'Well, actually my angels,' Mrs. Bannister said, 'the secret is this: you're always home, no matter where you are, because Now is home. Now is forever. N-O-W …' She sounded the word slowly, drawing it out for what seemed like an eternity. 'Remember this and you'll always be happy' [1]

One of the advantages of growing up in the years following the Second World War was the relative quiet. Roads were empty by today's standards, the motor car still a luxury. This was a time before mobile phones existed, when imaginative games and story books took the place of television and computers, and when time itself moved more slowly. Children were left very much to their own devices yet (in my experience at least), boredom never existed. There was only 'now,' an eternal moment filled with all kinds of

interesting possibilities. This was, and is, a definite advantage. It allows a child to become creative, self-aware, and independent; to discover his or her Inner Companion.
These qualities, fostered in childhood, serve us well throughout our lives.

Throughout her own life my mother suffered a good deal of ill health. She had lost her first child, Patrick, less than a year before I entered the world. Her early life had been harsh too. She was knocked down by a motor bike at the age of four. The eldest of six children, she was kept at home to look after the younger ones and in consequence fell behind with her studies. (In those days children were beaten for failing in their lessons). Her father was a skilled draughtsman and builder but his business failed when debtors refused to pay their bills. He turned to drink and on Friday nights my mother and the younger children lived in fear of his return after a night at the local public house.

My mother was naturally artistic but sadly her talents were overlooked and on leaving school at fourteen she was sent to work at a bootlace factory. Later she took a job as a home help for my father's family and when war broke out she drove trucks for the YMCA, delivering cigarettes and chocolate to the troops stationed nearby. She was a beautiful woman and had many invitations to the theatre from young officers. She often remarked that those war years were the happiest of her life.

My earliest memory of my father is of a man sitting on a hospital veranda in his dressing gown. He had returned from the war when I was nine months old and soon after suffered a severe mental breakdown and was subsequently hospitalised. The cause, he insisted, was a blow to the head – this undoubtedly because of the stigma attached to mental illness in those days.

He probably had a condition called 'shell shock,' now recognised as Post Traumatic Stress, due in part I am sure, to having been blown up in his Jeep. This he miraculously survived and later re-assembled his battalion, but meanwhile spent several terrifying weeks on the run from the Nazis in the forests of Northern France. Throughout much of his life he suffered from night terrors. Who knows what other dreadful wartime experiences may have haunted him?

The Inner Companion

My brother was born when I was four years old and our mother's health deteriorated over the years that followed. I was often afraid we might be orphaned and separated, especially when we were sent off to stay with different relatives from time to time. However, despite the upheaval of these enforced exiles there were also compensations. They encouraged me to rely on my own Inner Companion.

Naturally a rather solitary child I suppose discovered retreat quite early. I enjoyed a good deal of freedom, wandering the quiet Kentish lanes and savouring timeless moments that are every bit as real to me today. Sometimes I would visit St. Mary's at Horton Kirby, an ancient little church where my parents had married. Here I liked to reflect on the lives that had passed through its doors since Norman times, and often sat in the cold for hours, making brass rubbings and sketches of the interior.

For me this was a mystical place, filled with the scent of time-worn emptiness, and a silence I found compelling. It hinted at 'unseen worlds,' and a life that existed just beyond the ordinary.

I had already developed a dislike for organised religion, due mainly to the compulsory family visits to Sunday Matins and Evensong, times when all sense of mystery disappeared and silence gave way to the joyless voices of an elderly congregation ('Lone and dreary, faint and weary, through the desert Thou didst go ...'). Then the little church became dreary too, its pleasant mustiness overpowered by old Sunday suits and mothballs.

Now is Home

One summer when I was about eight years old I was sent to live with my maternal grandmother on the Essex coast. She was an unfeeling woman, worn out by years of child-rearing and frustration, and patently inconvenienced by my presence. She lived in a house near the sea, built on stilts as a protection against flooding. Each day I would walk for miles along the sea wall, preferring my own company to my grandmother's (whose feet, she reminded me, I was always under), oblivious to any dangers that might befall a small girl on her own.

Days and weeks passed and each night I longed for home. I was convinced that if I put my will to it I could leap from the bedroom window and fly safely back to my family. I kept hope alive by believing that it's possible to create whatever we need simply by thinking about it. However, I soon realised that the difficulty lay in the quality of that 'thinking.' Flying clearly required some very dedicated thought, something my own butterfly mind was as yet incapable of!

Fortunately, homesickness didn't get the better of me. Circumstances were developing in me a sense of independence, even courage – and again, a love of silence.

I think I have always felt ageless, neither young nor old, and discovered very early in life that we have within us all a place where we will always be safe. That place is 'now,' a timeless state that is our true home.

'Mind Quieting'

As I grew older I suffered a number of breakdowns – periods of acute anxiety, followed by chronic depression.

My childhood sense of 'now' was compromised by having to adapt to the world around me. Like many people I became temporarily absorbed with the demands of work, setting up home, and exploring new relationships.

Though I never completely lost sight of my Inner Companion and the 'unseen worlds,' I began to seek security, happiness (and especially love) in the outer world. Here, inevitably, I failed to find what I longed for.

It was only after a car accident in my thirties that a chain of events led me to practise meditation. For me this was Transcendental Meditation, which became widely known in the west during the late 1960s and early 1970s, due partly to the Beatles and the Beach Boys and their association with its guru and founder, Maharishi Mahesh Yogi. TM proved to be a very simple and 'safe' introduction to this natural and timeless human function.

It is said that there are as many meditation techniques as there are people. Any good practice will have a focus of some kind, a 'mind stilling' function that leads potentially to pure awareness. The emphasis may be on breathing, sound (a mantra or sacred word), contemplation, movement (Qigong, Tai Chi, Yoga, etc.), visual attention, or even the moment to moment perception of the present moment through mindfulness.

Meditation is a home-coming, a return to the Eternal Now, and therefore a retreat in itself.

Like retreat it too encourages restfulness, awareness, and self-compassion. Ultimately it creates 'inner companionship' – the vital link with our Inner Self. The following chapters will illustrate in detail how this can be achieved.

1 From *Now is Forever,* one of a collection of inspirational short stories called *The Last Post*

Part 2
On Retreat

Chapter Three
The Wordless Way

We wander far from home, led astray by false hopes and dreams. Yet one day we return, summoned by the Voice of the Silence

Welcome to *The Wordless Way*, our first pathway to retreat. We begin with a few moments of **Silent Sitting.** Remember, this will be a time of deep rest and healing; an act of kindness to yourself and to others.

Make sure you are fully awake and sitting upright if possible. Close your eyes and take a moment to raise your awareness to your 'High Place.' **(See Chapter One: Your Daily Routine)**.

Notice that you are breathing

Notice your breathing in ... and your breathing out. Relish each breath, knowing that it brings you closer to home, to your Inner Self.

Now notice your body
How does it feel? Is it resting or rest-less? Are there places in your body where you are holding on to tension? Allow your whole body to relax and become more peaceful.

Notice the sounds around you.
Enjoy the sounds of the outside world. Be peaceful and accepting of these sounds. There is no reason for them to disturb you.
Notice the inner sounds too - your thoughts
Accept these too without giving them any particular importance; they are just thoughts, the activity of a rest-less mind. There is no need for you to be distracted by them.

Once you feel steady and calm you will be ready to read your daily Message. Always read this with your heart, rather than your mind alone.
After your Message you will set your intention for today and make any notes.

Continue today and everyday, as outlined in **Chapter One**, ending with **The Evening Review**, a chance to reflect and prepare for sleep.

Day 1 - The Pathway of Silence

Welcome to the Wordless Way. Until further notice you are to follow the Way of Silence. This will do much to steady a spluttering and agitated mind, and bring peace to a troubled heart. Silence exists within sound. Even when you speak there is silence beyond your words. Understand the importance of silence in all you do today and experience its *vitality*. Rest, open and receive.
Notice how already in these first few moments of retreat, silence has changed you. In silence you become calm, compassionate, and mindful; a transmitter of Fiery Love.

Your Morning Resolve
When life could not be worse, when you feel you have lost everything, including hope, there is only one place left to go - inwards. Thus Silence calls you home.

The Still Centre within you is exactly the same Still Centre within me. It is the very same Centre of Consciousness to be found at the heart of all that exists.
This is a powerful thought indeed – for it means that we are all connected to everything in

existence, from the smallest to the largest life-form we can imagine.

Paradoxically silence isn't inert – it is teeming with creative energy and potential. Sense the healing power of silence at work within you right now! Feel the warmth of your Inner Fire as it soothes and sustains you, increases the very flow of your life force.

Embracing silence is an act of kindness to your self. You are responding to your own need for rest.

Whatever your resolve today, cultivate Silence at specific times throughout the day. Look for silence in everything – do not speak needlessly; instead, let there be silence behind your words and stillness in all your activities. You will consequently conserve your energy and become calm and peaceful. Draw today on the healing and creative qualities of Fire.

Rest, open, and receive: three simple rules of self-healing. Treat yourself with kindness and compassion and you will become a force of kindness and compassion in the world.

Day 2 - Stillness and Reverence:

Forget all that you have been taught about God. Until you have knelt at your own altar in stillness and reverence you have not found Me.

Your Morning Resolve

Never underestimate the power of Stillness. Silent Sitting is a sacred practice that brings us to the Life Within – the nearest we can come to an understanding of God, the Source of all that is.

For generations religious teachings have focussed on a distant God, unapproachable because of our sinful nature. We forget that the Divine is all that is (and therefore in everything and in all of us). We forget that Its essence is Love.

God is nearer than you think. Place a hand on your own heart; it's as simple as this.
And remember, you don't *have* an Inner Self – you *are* that Self! Draw on the transforming quality of Fire.

Enjoy moments of stillness today. Reflect on the mystery and magnificence of your own life, and the life of others. Draw on the illuminating quality of Fire. Kneel quietly at your own altar ...

Day 3 - My Silence

Seek not My Voice as proof of My Presence. Hear instead My Silence for that will tell you all you need.

Your Morning Resolve

This is the shortest of all the Messages and one of the most potent. It reminds us that the mind seeks answers and delights in analysis and evidence. If we can let go of this need for a while and - without any expectations – enjoy silence for its own sake, we experience our own Presence, rooted in our Inner Life. We are then open to the possibility of direct experience of the Divine. This is the flame that illuminates and heals.

Day 4 - Open and Receive

Let us go back to the beginning. You have been told to 'rest, open and receive.' Let us imagine that you are awaiting delivery of a parcel. You have been told that it will arrive very soon yet you wait for several days and still nothing comes.

Yet how can it, for you are never 'at home' to receive it.

So it is as you go about your business: planning and fretting, talking much and listening too little. For once, do nothing. Come home to your Silent Place and let the Gift be placed in your hands!

Your Morning Resolve

Come home! The Gift you long for is already there.

May this be your resolve today: firstly, to do nothing! Instead, *rest* (even if you are working). And as you rest, immerse yourself in the stillness of this present moment. Next, consciously soften your body. Notice any resistance and tension and soften a little more. Softening allows you to be receptive to the gifts of guidance and healing. It is your key to self-healing. Today be warmed by Fiery Love.

I count as blessings things I could have benefited from, even if I neglected to utilize them. A gift is still a gift, even if left wrapped and unopened.

Jarod Kintz, *Xazaqazax*

Day 5 - The Wordless Way

Be free from false comforts, free from the prettiness of words and the sweetness of affection. For how can sweetness and affection satisfy your soul?
Choose the simplicity of the Wordless Way: Silence.

Your Morning Resolve
False comforts come in many forms and include anything that reinforces our false sense of value in the world.
They include our human need for attention, for flattery, for romance; even the holding dear of rigid beliefs and opinions. All these belong to a fleeting world.
In silence we appreciate the deeper, enduring things of life, including our true self-worth.

Silence evokes the Eternal World where all that is superficial falls away and only Love remains. Communication at this level requires no words – it relies on the language of one heart to another.
As a writer I like to play with words, explore meanings, delve into origins; even create new ones. But I know that silence can often be more eloquent than language. Words inevitably fail us

when we seek to convey intangibles such as other-worldly experiences. Sometimes we convey more with our silence than with our words.
It is through *The Wordless Way* that we gain access to *intuition, healing, and unconditional love.*

Notice when your own silence is more articulate than your speech. Today, draw again on the illuminating power of Fire.
Resolve today to have silence behind all you say.

Day 6 – Fulfilment

Is there one thing left that you would do before the close of this life? Take time. Hear the silent longing of your heart for its highest fulfilment. Raise up the least of your desires …

Imagine yourself at the end of this, a long and eventful lifetime. Can you say, 'I have done all I came to do – and perhaps a little more'?

Your Morning Resolve

The search for happiness is deeply ingrained in us. We believe we *should* be happy, and if we're not then something has gone wrong; we must be somehow at fault. In the end the search is futile - happiness is fleeting since it depends on things going well. Far more important is the search for *meaning*. There is nothing like a sense of purpose to alleviate despair, depression and loneliness. Meaning and purpose guarantee a deeper sense of happiness: joy.

Let today be a time to reflect on your life so far – on what you have achieved, enjoyed and endured. Ponder too on those things you would still like to explore – ideas, inspirations, however small or

seemingly trivial. During your quiet moments draw on the creative power of Fire.
What would you like to do with the rest of your life?

Day 7 - Let this be your offering

Let the noise subside and the world fall silent.
Be as the Water Carrier and pour yourself into the world.
Baptise your body, mind and spirit from within.
Let this be your offering today.

Your Morning Resolve

Baptism symbolises a cleansing of body, mind and spirit. It also signifies initiation or entry – in this sense entry to the Life Within.
The ancient symbol of the Water Carrier shows one who kneels while pouring forth the Waters of Life. This is the act of service of a great spiritual being (the Universal Christ) towards humanity. According to the Ageless Wisdom teachings this divine offering carries the seeds of a new world order, namely the Brotherhood of Man, and with it the truth that we are all One.
In the Christian tradition the Waters of Life also bring the promise of Eternity.

Whenever we devote time to silence we become receptive to this Inner nurturance. Not only do we benefit ourselves but we are then able to offer ourselves in service to others.

This Message hints at the importance of being your Self. There is no one quite like you - there never has been, and never will be. Therefore your unique offering to the Whole is of immense value.

Remember this: day by day you make memories for others as well as yourself. By being 'you,' you make your mark on the world around you.
Therefore, never compare yourself with others, nor concern yourself with what they do. Draw on the purifying power of Fire and resolve only to be your Self today!

Day 8 - Coming Home

We wander far from home, led astray by false hopes and dreams. Yet one day we return, summoned by the Voice of the Silence.

Your Morning Resolve

In despair we are brought to our knees, having lost faith in the world, in ourselves, and in God. It is then that we find refuge once more in Silence.

Since life is never static we are wise to accept change as a natural feature of everyday life. There is great peace in accepting that change is inevitable. It is then possible to view impermanence as our teacher and guide. Such acceptance helps us to deal with difficult circumstances that afflict us from time to time.

Always remember the peaceful maxim: *this too will pass.* Become the Watcher - that part of you that witnesses both your suffering and your pleasure without preference. This Watcher heralds the stirrings of Awareness within you.

Today, may the Flame of Silence illuminate your passage. Remember also the transformative power of Fire and call your self home.

Chapter Four
Awareness

A Living Endless Eye,
Far wider than the Sky
Whose Power, whose Act, whose Essence was to see
(*The Preparative*, by Thomas Traherne)

When my father returned from the war towards the end of 1945 my mother and I had already moved from our temporary lodgings in the north of England to the family home in Kent.
Kent is only a short distance from London and because of its orchards and hop gardens is traditionally known as 'the Garden of England.' My father was born in Ireland and I was given a Celtic name, Moyra. I was brought up to believe in 'the little people,' (fairies, leprechauns and so on), a paradox really since he was also a very 'no nonsense' military man.

The Watcher

My most significant childhood memory - if not the earliest - is of waking up one night to find I was not alone. There, about eight feet above me, hovered a great 'Being of Light.'

It had no recognisable features but seemed to regard me with an intense but invisible 'all seeing eye.' I sensed that it had been there for some time, patiently observing me while I slept.

It looked on reflection like those curious medieval representations of angels, all head and no body.

If this Watcher was indeed an angel it wasn't the gentle and reassuring messenger one might expect. To my horror it appeared to know me through and through (I knew I couldn't escape its penetrating light), yet at the same time viewed me with disquieting indifference. I froze, mesmerised by its fiery brilliance and unable to make any sound. Then at last I found my voice. I let out a loud yell and my unexpected visitor took its leave, floating slowly away, to disappear finally through the window behind me. Hearing me, my mother appeared in the doorway and told me I must have had a bad dream. But it was no such thing, I knew for certain. Although I had no idea who had appeared that night or why, I had the distinct impression that someone was keeping a close eye on me.

As a small child I was often berated for being too introspective. I recall one morning standing in the dining room, looking out on the rain. 'Who is God?' I asked my mother. She didn't answer; the sounds from the kitchen told me she was attending to my baby brother. I persisted. 'And where is he?'

My mother came in from the kitchen and sat down. 'Up there,' she said, glancing upwards while spooning gripe water into my brother.
God, she elaborated, had a large black book in which he recorded everything I did, or even thought of doing. There was absolutely nothing he missed. Therefore, she inferred, I had better be good - or else suffer the consequences.

Now there was a nightmare! I didn't like the sound of this God at all. The Man in the Sky sounded extremely unpleasant, spying on people and thinking up punishments. I knew then at the age of four that I was already doomed!
My mother, of course, was repeating a myth passed down through the generations to keep

people on the straight and narrow (see **Message 2: Stillness and Reverence**). Years later I looked back on these two experiences of 'being watched.' Having rejected the Man in the Sky I was still eager to understand the identity of my very real night time visitor.

Today I know that despite its indifference, the 'Watcher' offered me a very pure kind of love; devoid of tenderness maybe, but unconditional and totally accepting. Regardless of its actual identity (my own Inner Self or some divine messenger) the Watcher symbolises for me the ever present *Indwelling God* inherent in each one of us, the very essence of our own nature.

Through careful self-watching we grow in Awareness and come to recognise various emotions and thought-forms that affect the way we live – e.g. our hopes, fears and expectations and how we react to other people.

It is only through *watching* (self-observation) that we begin to see how our difficulties arise from well-worn patterns of thinking, old trauma, and unresolved grievances.

These tendencies prevent us from seeing life as it really is, and thus make up our illusory world of Glamour.

Glamour and the importance of watching

Glamour is a rather archaic word suggestive of magic and enchantment. It is a form of illusion and refers to anything that clouds our vision. Glamour causes us to view life – and especially ourselves – through a dense emotional mist which only the light of our Inner Life can illuminate and dispel **(see Introduction: The Nature of Fire**).

Glamour arises from our conditioning and includes those false ideas and beliefs that we take on as a result of past experience.

How then do we discern what is real? Only by persistently *watching,* with a real desire for truth. For some it may take an 'other-worldly' phenomenon (an out-of body or near death experience, vision, etc.) to reveal the difference between ordinary and ultimate reality. People who have such experiences report an indescribable clarity of knowing that overshadows the lesser reality of everyday life.

Glamour exists when we identify with our emotions and are controlled by them. Uncontrolled emotion potentially causes immense harm to our selves and others.

The greatest of glamours is the universal belief in separation. This illusion fuels every selfish human desire and is responsible for all forms of thoughtless and destructive behaviour.

It is by developing Awareness that we free ourselves from the illusion of the separate self and discover that ultimately we all share the same essence. This beautiful truth is emphasised throughout the world's religions and spiritual philosophies: *treat other people as you would wish to be treated yourself.*

Developing Awareness through The Seven Rays

According to the Ageless Wisdom teachings there are seven cosmic streams of energy that condition all life on earth. These are known as *The Seven Rays of Life.* For our own solar system these energies have their origin in seven Great Lives, embodied by seven stars in the constellation of The Great Bear. Each stream of energy has a particular quality and all forms of life are said to be coloured by one or other of them – our solar system, planet, nations, plants, animals and, not least ourselves, humanity.

I include The Seven Rays here, not as a belief system to be followed, but to illustrate the possibility of various cosmic forces that, like astrology, may exert influence upon our nature. If we consider the impact of such forces upon us we end up with a complex and fascinating picture; a rainbow of qualities that result in the unique human being that each one of us is.

In short, it is said that the ray governing our Inner Life or soul remains constant through each lifetime, whereas those rays influencing our personality, mind, emotions and body tend to change from life to life. Through the process of rebirth we evolve, learning life's lessons along the way via the diverse experiences each ray gives us.

We are essentially *souls in incarnation,* evolving human beings whose task is to express the qualities of our Soul Ray more perfectly.

Ray Types (Virtues and Vices)

Although Rays 2, 4 and 6 offer ready contact with our Inner Life (Rays 1, 3, 5 and 7 facilitating greater ease of contact with the material world), no one ray is better than another, nor is any one ray more spiritual. The same can be said of the twelve signs of the zodiac, each one being a perfect expression of divinity.

The Inner Life only expresses a ray's virtues whereas the personality largely exhibits its vices or glamours. (A vice is simply a ray quality that is distorted or imperfectly expressed). Through self-awareness and increased identification with our Inner Life we can learn to transform our particular shortcomings into strengths.
To give you an example of this, I identify strongly with Ray 2 and to a certain extent, Ray 6. When I am operating from my soul I am able to express the Ray 2 qualities of love, endurance, serenity, intuition, and so on. However, the shadow side of my personality will more often than not display Ray 2 coldness, selfishness, impatience, anxiety, plus some of the negative aspects of Ray 6, particularly anger.

Below is an abbreviated list of the seven 'ray types' and their qualities.[1] A glance at these will quickly reveal those needing to be developed or transmuted in each case. What do you intuitively recognise as predominant 'virtues' and 'vices' in yourself?

Ray 1: Will - Power
Virtues: Courage, leadership, single-mindedness, etc.
Vices: Ruthlessness, arrogance, ambition, tyranny, cruelty, etc.

Ray 2: Love-Wisdom
Virtues: Endurance, divine love, serenity, intuition, truth, etc. Vices: Coldness, selfishness, impatience, anxiety, love of being loved, suspicion, etc.

Ray 3: Active Intelligence
Virtues: Philosophical attitude - ability to think in an abstract way; clear intellect, sincerity.
Vices: Intellectual pride, deviousness, inaccuracy, absent-mindedness, busyness.

Ray 4: Harmony through Conflict
Virtues: Affection, sympathy, courage, generosity, quickness of intellect.
Vices: Self-centeredness, worrying, inaccuracy, cowardice/moral weakness, extravagance.

Ray 5: Concrete Knowledge or Science
Virtues: Keen intellect, accuracy, perseverance, common sense, uprightness.
Vices: Harsh criticism, narrowness, arrogance, un-forgiveness, lack of sympathy, prejudice.

Ray 6: Idealism or Devotion
Virtues: Devotion, single-mindedness, love, intuition, loyalty, sympathy.
Vices: Selfishness, jealousy, sentimentality, fanaticism, anger.

Ray 7: Ceremonial Order
Virtues: Strength, self-reliance, perseverance, courage, courtesy, meticulousness, creativity.
Vices: Formalism, bigotry, pride, narrowness, poor judgment, superstition.

A study of the Seven Rays (and indeed astrology) can increase our intuition as well as help us develop strengths and remedy weaknesses. It will also highlight our various human differences and explain why it is we relate more to some Ray 'types' than to others (i.e. those who share a similar 'ray structure' to our own, and the difficulties we may have with those who don't)!

In short, an understanding of the Rays will inspire self-awareness, not in a neurotic way but positively and ideally, with good humour. In fact, when we learn to take ourselves less seriously we might even begin to enjoy the process of self-transformation! **(Chapter Five: Healing and Transformation)**

There now follows a new 8-day period of retreat during which we shall practise the simple art of 'noticing.'

1 My brief introduction cannot possibly do justice to this vast and complex science. For a detailed study of this subject I recommend, along with other books by the same author, *Esoteric Psychology Vol. 1*, given by the Master D.K. through Alice A. Bailey and *The Seven Rays of Life*, a compilation of Alice A. Bailey's work. Both are published by the Lucis Trust.

Day 9 – Breathe

Breathe … and know that you are breathing. Understand, for now and always, the significance of this moment. *Know that you are Life itself.*
All else proceeds from this.

Your Morning Resolve
This is Awareness at its most basic – an awareness of life itself; something we are reminded of each time we breathe consciously. Breathing (really *knowing* you are breathing), calms emotions, restores energy and brings you fully into this one eternal moment – *now*.

Resolve today to pause and notice. Breathe with awareness throughout the day, especially when you are tired or struggling with pain or anxiety. Draw on the illuminating power of Fire and become the Watcher of all you think and do.

Day 10 - Breath of Life

Let breath come to you. How easy, how beautiful a breath is. Breathe … Your breath is a symbol of life's renewal. Open and receive the Breath of Life.

Your Morning Resolve

Breathing with awareness is fundamental to our well-being and for this reason we return to this simple practice each day. Resolve to enjoy each breath (your breathing in ... and your breathing out ...) whenever you can. This reminds us to take time, to be in no rush. The health benefits are manifold – from relieving stress, exhaustion and insomnia to normalising heart rate and blood pressure. Notice how quickly you feel renewed when you breathe with awareness. It brings an immediate increase in the 'subtle breath' or vital force, known variously as Prana, Chi or Qi. This is the Breath of Life. Such is the healing power of Fire.

Day 11 – Refuge

How difficult it is for you to settle when your mind is on fire! It burns unchecked, producing heat and agitation in the body, causing the nervous system to fire unsteadily. Return to your place of refuge and let your mind be a steady light. Breathe and sound the sacred word. Rest and know that all is well.

Your Morning Resolve

In ancient systems such as Ayurveda excess fire in the body is regarded as a cause of inflammation and disease. It is believed that certain foods will aggravate fire and should be eliminated from the diet in favour of those that 'cool' the system, something that is gaining acceptance in the West. Apart from diet we are also discovering that many chronic inflammatory conditions such as asthma and eczema can be eased by mindful techniques.

This Message invokes the healing power of Fire. It also urges us to sound the sacred word, OM. This mantra (sounded silently or thought), reconnects us with the Source of all Life and is something we can practise at any time.

Resolve today to return often to your refuge. Be aware, moment to moment, of the connection between your thoughts and your body. Again, become the Watcher. Breathe, rest and let your mind be a steady light.

Day 12 – Furtherance

Your key word today is *Furtherance.* Begin to put into action those plans that have lain dormant for a while. It is time to begin a period of training. Take time each day to reflect on your plans, to develop ideas and receive inspiration.

Your Morning Resolve

This Message has echoes of **Day 6: Fulfilment.** *What would you like to do with the rest of your life?* Your 'period of training' is not intended to be burdensome. It is a time of respite to be welcomed; a time for heightened awareness, creative ideas and inspiration.

Use your Silent time to reflect on any unfulfilled dreams or unfinished projects ...

- New places to visit
- A room to decorate or a cupboard to tidy
- Books to read (or even a book to write)
- A letter to compose - long intended - to a friend
- A new hobby or course to begin
- A change of career

What would it take to make your dreams come true? Consider some simple life-style changes to take your plans further. Notice any doubts that come to mind, thoughts that sabotage or delay your intentions.

Resolve today to take one small project, however mundane, and develop it. Be open and flexible to all new ideas. Even small steps forward can bring great satisfaction. Such is the creative power of Fire.

Day 13 - Act Now!

Act now – or will you wait until you are in better health or a better mood? Until you have more time or fewer commitments? Will you hold back until you have found the answers to all your problems, until your pain or loneliness have passed? Until you have found the right job or the perfect partner? Will you wait until you are no longer afraid? How long will you wait?
Actually you will never be in a better place or at a more auspicious time than Now. Act now!

Your Morning Resolve
This Message continues yesterday's theme of Creative Fire and reminds us that we will find many excuses for avoiding change! Notice what these are. We so easily delay; afraid of failure maybe, afraid even of success – who knows?

New attitudes and resolutions take time to implant and require constant attention and nurturing. Any course of action demands *fire* – and fire can be both destructive and creative. The old ways (ideas, beliefs, habits) have first to be cleared to make room for the new. So, ask yourself: *What stands in my way? What is holding me back?* Notice!

My father began to write a book in old age. It was a wonderful account of how co-incidence played such a huge part in his life, particularly during the War years. He had so many fascinating and miraculous stories to share but sadly he left it all too late. He had already developed Parkinson's disease, a condition that eventually made writing impossible.

One of my friend Bob's favourite expressions was 'tick, tock!'* He was only too aware that life is short and we shouldn't waste it. Many times we are moved by a great idea but then talk ourselves out of it, or fail to summon enough will to see it through.

I wonder how many books are still waiting to be written, how many great ideas shelved.

All I can say is this:
May your resolve today be to *Act Now*!
If you have a passion – an idea that grabs you, an initiative that may benefit others, a work project, or some special journey to make – begin it, NOW! Tick tock.

*(*Take Me to the Mountain: discovering the you that never dies*)

Day 14 - Awareness

Do not be petty in your dealings with others but meticulous in your handling of yourself. Recognise the strength and capacity of your own personality! See also its weakness – the little chinks in its armour. Do not dwell on these little flaws but instead hold your attention high, as always, and allow the Light of Awareness to do its work in you.

Your Morning Resolve

Self-awareness is the ability to *see* our strengths and weaknesses with equal clarity and compassionate detachment. Compassion is vital. This is why it is so important to change our perspective and keep our attention 'high.' (**See Chapter One: Your Daily Routine**). Yet it's so much easier, isn't it, to divert attention from our own imperfections and find fault with others? It somehow eases our discomfort.

Again, become the Watcher! *Notice* when others 'press your buttons.' Buttons are meant to be pressed! They too are our teachers. There is a divine magnetic rapport between our weaknesses and wounds and those who offend us. In a strange and mysterious way that magnetic connection is Love. Fiery Love both warms and destroys, and seen from a higher perspective it brings us awareness, balance and healing. Just 'noticing' creates this change.

So, let this be your resolve today: observe yourself, not in a neurotic and self-conscious way but with poise and compassion. *Notice!*

Day 15 - The Lighted Way

Whether you know it or not, you are on a journey of discovery, one which will eventually lead you to the Lighted Way, the Way of Revelation. But how often do you walk, your eyes downcast, and focus on the little things of life? Or do you sometimes raise your gaze to the night sky and wonder at the worlds beyond worlds that you see there, tiny points of light that in truth are brighter than a thousand suns? Do you then pause and ask your self: *Who am I exactly? And what am I doing here?*
Oh, how easy it is to forget!

Your Morning Resolve
This Message alerts us once more to a change of perspective, and illumination. Despite our difficulties, it reminds us to keep our attention high and *see the bigger picture.*

Who are you? Why are you here? Call upon the illuminating power of Fire. Be inquisitive and ask yourself these questions often. Today, regard your Life as a journey of discovery: become the child who never stops seeing the magic in life.

Day 16 – Change

Your patient observation of yourself and unflinching acceptance of *all you see* is clarifying your view of yourself and the world. Now is a time of increased spiritual opportunity and of attendant change. Your very seeing of yourself creates that change.

Your Morning Resolve

Patience is paramount at every stage of our journey – patient observation, patient detachment, patient compassion. All these increase our awareness and understanding of ourselves and the world we live in. So too with acceptance, the fruits of which take us to the next Pathway: *Healing and Transformation.*

Everything in your Life Story takes you further – all your heartaches and difficulties have the potential to bring you new understanding, and therefore acceptance. Whatever happens, always ask yourself: *What is the lesson in this?*

Today, see the fiery effects of illumination and transformation in your life. More than ever, be the Watcher and resolve to see opportunities in everything you encounter. Healing always involves change.

Chapter Five
Healing & Transformation

Speak your need to Me now.
Your need for guidance, love, freedom from pain.
What is your need?
Ask and it is already given.
For you are that guidance, that love, that freedom.
You are the divinity you seek.
You are My Hands, My Feet, My Voice.
You are My Eyes and My Ears.
You are all to Me, My Healing Presence.

(From: Take Me to the Mountain: discovering the you that never dies)

In tackling such a vast and mysterious subject as healing there is always a danger of slipping into platitudes – reassuring aphorisms whose value and effectiveness become lost through overuse.
To heal (Old English *haelen*) means to make whole or sound. Left to its own devices, the

body/mind/spirit (the complete human being) is ever seeking to 'repair' itself and restore a state of equilibrium and wholeness. This repair process may paradoxically manifest through illness - and even death.

Death is sometimes known as *The Great Healer* (**See Day 24: The Great Healer**) since it eliminates the cause of disease (cf. the purging, transformative effect of Fire).

No one is completely healthy all of the time. Health is relative and having a healthy body doesn't necessarily guarantee a life free from suffering. Disease (*dis-ease*) is really an interruption in the flow of Life and has various causes – hereditary, psychological, environmental, or karmic, etc. Whatever the cause, our first task is to determine the source of our suffering, and then seek its remedy.

Healing and Transformation always go hand in hand since healing inevitably requires change of some kind – a change in thinking based on new understanding, a change of lifestyle, a change of heart. From this perspective the process of healing ultimately involves a good deal of Self-discovery and Self-mastery.

True healing, as opposed to the temporary relief of symptoms or circumstances, is only ever possible through the agency of our Inner Self or Soul, that part of us that is beyond pain and suffering. Sickness occurs when we are cut off from this Self. Therefore, anything that can lead us back to our Self will ultimately encourage healing. Whatever the nature of our suffering – whether in body, mind or spirit - it is again wise to look for the source of the problem, and very often the cause will be found within the mind itself. **The purpose of each daily Message is to create a space in which change, and thereby healing, can occur.**

A Gift of Grace

Sometimes healing is mysteriously spontaneous and entire in its effect – that is to say, it gets directly to the underlying cause of the condition. We call this miracle healing. When such healing occurs it feels like a gift of Grace and we are left in no doubt that healing is complete.

There are many well-documented cases of miracle cures. One such is the subject of Anita Moorjani's book, 'Dying to be Me.' [1] Ms Moorjani describes how, at the point of death, she was made inwardly aware of two important facts. Firstly, that a certain attitude of mind was the root cause of her then 'terminal' illness, and secondly that she would be completely cured should she decide to return to her body. Her incredible Near Death Experience and subsequent return to full health have not only transformed her own life but inspired her to share her experience with others.

Healing is an act of Love. It makes sense therefore that we begin to love our wounds and seek to understand the reason for their existence. What for instance might suffering tell us about ourselves, our beliefs; our fears? What might we change in the way we live our lives?
Everything that happens to us is potentially there to bring us back to ourselves – and is in this sense a gift. Good things, and not so good things, are all signs if we are aware enough to discern them.

Life constantly offers us clues to help us solve our problems, and heal our dis-ease. However, unless we are vigilant and receptive to the wisdom of our Inner Life, we tend to miss these subtle hints.

Therefore, never run from your *feelings* – instead notice them, listen to them compassionately, for they will develop your intuition and show you where healing is most needed, where changes need to be made.

Maybe you are worrying about something that is out of your control, afraid that your pain will never lessen and only get worse. Perhaps you are anxious for tomorrow, or distressed about the past, grieving for something lost. All these are signs that you have temporarily lost your connection with your Inner Life, the part of you that is not attached to circumstances. The part of you that knows ultimately *all is well*, and that this lifetime is just a very brief episode in a far greater Life Story. Each feeling of distress is a signal, pointing you back to this Self, where nothing can harm you, where all is well.

We shall look again at the role of signs, symbols and timely messages that remind us that our difficulties are both known and understood and are all part of a cycle of healing and transformation (**Day 18: All is Well**).

Discovering Healing

My own introduction to healing began officially in 1984. I say 'officially' because it is sometimes difficult to pinpoint exactly when an awakening or realisation takes place. The truth is often more subtle, part of a process that begins much earlier than we may be aware of.

As I child I was always curious about Life and its origins and purpose, aware that there are great mysteries beyond the edge of our vision. Children are still close to the subtle worlds so these instincts are natural to them.

I began to search for books that might provide answers but in those days there was little information available to the young seeker; no Body, Mind, Spirit sections in book shops and public libraries, no internet to consult.

In 1964 I was fortunate to win a student scholarship to Paris where I had a chance meeting with a young Frenchman who belonged to the modern day version of an ancient mystery school, the Rosicrucian Order. This particular branch of esoteric philosophy held some fascination for me at the time. He introduced me to meditation and various occult practices of mind control. I learned more about the theory of reincarnation (something I knew of instinctively as a child), a certainty that was reinforced by various past-life experiences I was having at that time.

Some years later **(Chapter Two)** I discovered Transcendental Meditation and later still, a branch of Buddhism known then as the Western Buddhist Order (now the Triratna Community). I was by this time a teacher and was very disillusioned with the limitations of our education system. I longed to find a new direction for my work. I had already a sense of my own calling as a healer but was as yet unsure how best to pursue it, especially as training was both expensive and time consuming. A colleague who shared my concerns was a Spiritualist and suggested that I might be interested in learning Reiki, a healing method that had recently come to the UK. The only Reiki training centre I could find at that time was in London. (This was in the mid-1980s before Reiki became as well known as it is today.) I trained with American Reiki Master, Joseph Porter, and practised on colleagues and friends for several years before formally setting up my own healing practice in the 1990s. In 1995 I decided to broaden my knowledge of healing and completed the Healing Diploma course at the College of Healing in Malvern.

Becoming a Healing Presence

Since human beings are natural healers training can only refine what is already innate. (Needless to say, it is only when healing is practised professionally that qualifications become necessary.) We all have the capacity to heal and the best way is to begin with ourselves. For me, the simplest yet most powerful forms of healing involve Healing Presence and Healing Prayer.

Healing Presence is a way of life. **(See Messages 23: The Great Healer, 25: My Blessing, and 34: We are One)**. It deepens our sense of connection with all living beings – plants, animals, other people, and the earth itself. In practising Healing Presence, we recognise that we not only have a profound effect on others but are inextricably linked with them.

Healers do nothing of themselves. They - we - are simply channels for a Greater Healing Power, however this is perceived. Healing therefore requires that we attune to this power (depending on the individual this may mean God, Universal Energy, an angel, a spiritual guide, etc.). Next, we

acknowledge our own sacredness, and that same sacred essence in others. (This is the meaning behind the respectful Sanskrit greeting *Namaste* or *Namaskar*).
To heal we need to develop unconditional acceptance and compassion ('feeling with') for the person involved. Whether that person is you or someone else is irrelevant. In fact, it is always beneficial to regard everyone you encounter as another 'you.'

Healing is much more than the laying on of hands. Your voice, your intent, the way you view others, your thoughts and prayers – all these are healing tools.

Healing Prayer
Another very simple but powerful practice is Distant or Absent Healing, in which prayers are offered with the intention to relieve suffering.

When we are troubled or in pain it can be difficult to meditate or settle to prayer. It is then that we can ask others to act on our behalf. Conversely, praying for others will often alleviate or distract us from our own suffering. **(See also: Helping others is good for you; Day 23: The Great Healer; Day 25: My Blessing; and Day 28: Trust.)**

The usefulness of prayer has so far proved difficult to measure in scientific trials but has substantial anecdotal support. In case you have any doubts about the effectiveness of Healing Prayer, do take a look at Dr. Larry Dossey's integrative approach to healthcare, and in particular his book *Healing Words: The Power of Prayer and the Practice of Medicine* (Published by Harper Collins 1993).[2]

Healing Circles

Healing Prayer is greatly magnified when undertaken in groups (Healing Circles). The practice is similar but varies according to the individuals concerned. It is usually led by one of the group. **(See Chapter Seven)**

Helping others is good for you

Medical scientists have begun to discover what many of us know instinctively: that voluntarily helping others is beneficial to our own health. (I add the word voluntarily because I believe it to be significant. Service performed from duty alone, perhaps with resistance or resentment, will inevitably have a reverse effect).

Psycho-neuro-immunology (PNI), investigates the power of the mind to influence health and healing. PNI research has produced some interesting results. IgA is an antibody involved in the body's defence against infection. Harvard psychologist, Dr David McClelland, measured IgA levels in a group of students before and after watching a film about Mother Teresa's work with the homeless. He found that by simply watching a film about selfless service the students' immune systems were already strengthened significantly.[3]

We can always be of selfless service to others, even when we are ill, bedridden or debilitated. We need only to 'retreat,' remembering that nothing is required of us other than our intention to be of help. An open heart and a simple request for assistance is all, for Love is the force behind all healing. This works as much for ourselves and our own healing as it does for others. If only more of us could recognise and apply this simple act, our world would certainly be a better place.

There are many stories of those who have suffered devastating loss, only to become motivated to use their grief in a positive way – helping others and consequently relieving their own suffering in the process. Compassion prevents us from being too absorbed in ourselves.

When we reach out to other people we automatically feel less alone: and being concerned with relieving the pain of our fellow beings, we retrieve a sense of purpose and common humanity.

I never cease to be amazed by the power of prayer and the practice of so-called 'distant' or 'absent' healing. The beauty of such practices lies in their simplicity and reliance on Love. When Love is the intention miracles can and do happen! A focussed, loving thought will cross barriers of time and distance (hence the misnomers 'distant' and 'absent') and touch the minds and hearts of those prayed for. Love is the great link between all forms of life and most certainly between the healing channel and the one who receives. Healing is a partnership in which all receive healing, all benefit.

1 Dying to be Me: My Journey from Cancer, to Near Death, to True Healing
(Hay House 2012 ISBN 9781781800140)

2 Dr Larry Dossey: www.dosseydossey.com

3 www.heartmath.com

Day 17 – Goodness

The abundance and goodness inherent in Nature is also within you. Imagine a garden, sown with your own seed thoughts. Take time to tend those thoughts that are healthy, while weeding out those that destroy the beauty and harmony of your true Nature.

Your Morning Resolve

Today's Message focuses on purging and creating. Retreat is a time for clearing and healing but this process cannot proceed if we continue to overload our system with toxins; hence the need for vigilance. This means not only adopting a healthy diet but a healthy attitude too.[1] How do we achieve this when we are, after all, only human? Firstly through Silence which, in turn, reinforces our powers of observation; then through Awareness – awareness of the incredible power of thought and its effect on our body and our mood.

As we recognise this fact more and more – the lifting or lowering of mood according to the thoughts that preoccupy us – we may conclude that *whatever we focus on* creates yet more of the same and conditions the life we live. Such is the creative power of Fire. It makes sense then to give patient attention to what we think.

Imagine the Garden of your Life. What do you find there - a place of peace and harmony, regardless of the changing seasons? A pleasant, colourful place that others are drawn to - or somewhere dismal, neglected and overgrown? What has taken root in your garden?

A beautiful garden doesn't appear by accident. It is the result of dedicated effort - hours of patient digging, weeding and pruning; joyful sowing and tending of new seeds. So it is with your Life.
Spend a little time in your 'garden' today. *Notice* those 'seed thoughts' that disturb your peace of mind and cause havoc in your body. Do a little digging. Weed out any thoughts that harm: bitter, jealous, critical, suspicious, guilty, anxious, and self-pitying thoughts. Yes, especially self-pity, something we have all indulged in, even fleetingly, especially in times of suffering. Self-pity is perfectly understandable but it can also be addictive. It is the mark of a victim, someone who needs our loving compassion, yet firm encouragement to stand confidently alone.

I'm sure you know those who talk endlessly of their suffering and misfortune; or conversely, others who mutely soldier on, rejecting all offers of help. You may offer advice, suggest useful remedial action, tried and tested practices - but all to no avail. A Victim will find all kinds of excuses for not taking action. 'It's difficult for me. Nothing works.' These beliefs are impenetrable defences that virtually nothing will breach.

He will often wear his suffering as a badge. One that tells the world 'No one can possibly understand because no one suffers as I do.' Although apparently passive, he will persist relentlessly to get what he wants - usually attention, energy. Victimhood is self-centred.

And for those who are caught up in rescuing the Victim, there is only exhaustion, unhappiness, and a sense of having failed. You offer a lifeline and your Victim will sit clinging to his self-pity.

Often there is another badge that goes with Victimhood: 'It doesn't matter about me.' This announces either a complete absence of self-worth and self-respect,
or the very opposite: the thinly disguised conviction that actually his needs are paramount. Behind this belief is a fiery rage.

There is a stubborn arrogance associated with Victimhood. We may even recognise ourselves as the Victim from time to time!

Be a skilful gardener and undertake your weeding and pruning cheerfully, even with a sense of amusement. Try not to take yourself too seriously today but proceed with loving compassion instead.

And remember to go into Nature whenever you can, especially if you are blessed with a garden of your own. Enjoy the view from your window. Nature teaches us that all things pass; and just as the seasons change, so do our circumstances.
Notice the flow of hope and wellbeing within you as you begin to foster positive, compassionate thoughts. *All is well.*

1 Research indicates that whenever we are stressed our energy reserves are distracted from their work of regenerating and repairing the body. We can avoid this cellular 'starvation' by focussing on positive thoughts and feelings (caring, appreciation and *love*) that nourish the body, right down to our cells and even to the level of DNA
See the work of biologist and author Bruce Lipton, and the HeartMath Institute:
www.brucelipton.com
www.heartmath.org

Day 18 - All is well

Welcome all set-backs as they come. They bring opportunities for measured thought and emotional poise. It is beneficial to be 'set-back' from time to time for then you see the value of detachment.
A set-back heralds a period of reflection and seeing things anew.
So, be at peace with your frustration. Be at peace with disappointment, and keep your attention higher still. All is well. Do you sense how profound this is? *All is well.*

Your Morning Resolve
Recently I was engaged in a telephone consultation with a young woman who has a painful and life-limiting condition. She was very despondent that day and asked me to lead her through a meditation, in the hope it might lighten her mood. Tears were very near the surface. What she sought most was relief from the unbearable sadness and frustration she felt, imprisoned as she is in a body that refuses to co-operate with her. At that moment, her life was one big set-back.

I knew she needed some kind of reassurance and though anxious to avoid platitudes, was confident that one of the Messages would help her that day. Something that would remind her that, despite all her difficulties, all is well.
Blindly, I allowed my free hand to seek out a card on her behalf from the pack. Imagine my delight – and hers – when this Message appeared. *All is Well.*

Today, welcome any set-backs, any unexpected interruptions to your plans. They may well be blessings in disguise. Even illness or accidents can later be viewed as beneficial in that they create much needed periods of rest and withdrawal.
Times that we would otherwise deny ourselves. Sometimes we are called to pause; to do nothing; to see things differently. This is the illuminating power of Fire.

Our sense of self-worth is so dependent on achievement that we often forget the value of (so-called) failure. As a general rule we learn more by 'failing' than succeeding. This applies to all areas of our lives: relationships, education, work, creative projects. Virtually anything we have expectations attached to. 'Failure' helps us to recognise our strengths and weaknesses, and teaches us what works, and what (or who) needs to be avoided in future. Failure also keeps complacency in check and fosters humility. As poet and lyricist, Stephen Kalinich, reminds us:

The greatest way to success is to be prepared for failure, to not rely on outcomes for your joy but on inner resources. The real success is he who can lose everything and be not disappointed, who feels good in spite of circumstance.

Signs on the Path

Being 'set-back,' you may feel uncertain of which way to turn. For now, do nothing. Instead, be vigilant and follow the signs. Signs will always appear, often in unexpected ways - a chance meeting or conversation, a book or television programme that gives direction and guidance.

Many years ago I was going through a period of personal upheaval. I needed guidance and didn't know which way to turn. Then one day I returned home to find a number of twigs arranged as if by intent on the path leading to my front door. Instinctively I had an immediate sense of alarm. They had clearly not been scattered randomly by the wind but were definite patterns: hieroglyphs, three separate symbols placed carefully by some unseen hand. Who on earth had taken the trouble to leave me this, as yet, incomprehensible message? Nervously, I copied the symbols into my notebook and pondered on them later. I wondered if they might be Runic symbols, something of which I then knew little but subsequently developed a great interest in. Sure enough, a little research showed they were just that – three Runic letters[1] which, when read from right to left, conveyed a specific message relating to my situation, together with the advised action, and finally, the most desirable outcome.

I never did discover who or what had been responsible for the message on my path that day but it was indeed timely. Although it warned of a further period of suffering (hence my initial alarm) it also brought me comfort because I knew it was all part of an unavoidable cycle of transformation from which I would eventually emerge.

You may well have had similar signs upon your 'path' - experiences of timely messengers, chance meetings, information that comes to you at exactly the right time, unexpected words of hope and encouragement, or some undeniable experience of a loved one who has passed, affirming that death does not exist.

All these serve to remind us that *All is Well.*
Relax, take comfort, and submit to the transformative power of Fire.

1 *The Book of Runes* Ralph Blum (ISBN 0747208964 Headline Book Publishing 1993)

Day 19 - The Wounded Healer

Deep within your joy may be an uprising of doubt or anxiety. Do not push discomforts aside but observe their source: memories of loss, past errors and regrets, shadows of lessons not yet learned. Face all of these calmly, without excuses or sorrow. Face all you have done, and all you have been, with a steady and loving gaze. See only the pain you once caused yourself.
Now let it all go, with the certainty that a lesson has been well-learned. It was all training for higher work!

Your Morning Resolve
I think there is within us all the knowledge that joy and sorrow coexist. We have only to look back on the course of our own lives and see that all things pass, everything runs according to cycles. Just as this brings comfort in times of difficulty, it can be alarming to realise that when life is easy, it is also unlikely to last! The answer lies always in non-attachment. This is the ability to view life exactly as it is, regardless of our circumstances. And even while enjoying the goodness of life, to be no more lost in pleasure than in pain.

The Wounded Healer is a perfect message to ponder on during your Evening Review. Apart from being a good exercise in observation and detachment it also reminds us of our need for self-compassion.

If you are caught up in a cycle of regret, consider that you don't need to hold onto to guilt forever. Guilt serves a purpose of course – it teaches us responsibility for our actions; shows us that what we do – or don't do – affects others and ourselves equally, because 'we are one another' in essence. This in itself is a priceless lesson.

The Wounded Healer is a call to Unconditional Love – a gentle reminder to love your 'self,' for all you are, all you were, and all you ever will be. Be warmed by the healing power of Fire.
Paradoxically our wounds ultimately heal and enlighten us. And just as failure may teach us more than success, wounds prepare us for beneficial service to others. After all, we teach best from personal experience and the more errors made, and suffering endured, the more we can relate compassionately to others.

Day 20 - Consequence

Shall we consider the role of consequence in our lives? Consequence teaches us to be awake to the choices we make; to choose thoughtfully and wisely. Consequence is our moment-to-moment creation.

Your Morning Resolve

This message touches on the Law of Cause and Effect, known in the East as Karma. Even if we don't believe in Karma, we instinctively recognise it as 'what goes around, comes around.' It is reflected in the New Testament quotation 'as you sow, so shall you reap,' a Law that reminds us, moment to moment, that we are responsible for, and creators of, our own lives. That is to say: every thought, word and action is energy; a living creation that carries a particular vibration. These vibrations eventually return to us as positive or negative conditions, according to their original quality. Our task then is to understand the creative potential of our minds and to use it wisely. Remember the Garden of your Life **(Day 17)**.

Today's resolve is to approach each thought, each spoken word, and each action with loving kindness. Be aware of moment to moment choices and draw on the Creative Power of Fire.

Day 21 - Harvest

The unfolding of karmic conditions arises in cycles, cycles that may be shorter or longer periods of time. It is necessary to accept the harvest of karma, to be unflinching and patient. So, welcome all difficulties as a means of clearing the old and making way for the new.

Your Morning Resolve

It is important to state here that Karma is not punishment, nor are its effects necessarily inescapable.[1] (Indeed it is sometimes said that once a lesson is fully learned the resulting change of heart and redirection of thought may offset karmic conditions.)

Karma is neutral and accounts for much of the good and bad that we are experiencing in our lives today - the result of our actions, positive or negative, recent or ancient.
We bring over from past lifetimes some of the very conditions that we experience today. All actions create reactions and for every effect that occurs in our lives there is a specific cause. Therefore, if we are unhappy with the effects we are experiencing it is wise to consider the possible

causes, known or unknown, and resolve to change for the better the way we live our lives *now.* In this way we create more favourable conditions for the future – or what we call 'good karma.'

The Law of Cause and Effect is an exact Law and far more complex than personal karma alone. It concerns the whole of our planetary existence. We have to remember that we do not live in isolation; our own lives are inextricably linked with humanity as a whole. This is the significance of the statement: We are One. Every action and interaction has its effect on the whole and thus we are subject not only personal karma but to group karma too. Thus, karmic conditions originating from humanity itself (of which we are a part), will also affect us.

Whatever the cause of our current circumstances we can if we choose, change our thinking from 'I hate my life, I wish I had an easier time of it' to 'I am blessed with this special opportunity to burn off a great load of karma, created over lifetimes.' Like death, karma can also be viewed as The Great Healer. Once a cycle of karma is accepted with good grace, lived through, and learned from, that cycle is completed.

Karma is not always the cause of illness. It may be instead that the soul has chosen limitations as a means of developing attributes such as humility, patience, endurance or compassion.

Whatever the cause of our personal difficulties, our resolve today is to live harmlessly and compassionately so that we no longer continue to create negative conditions for ourselves and for others. Today, as you draw on the Purging and Transforming Power of Fire, approach yourself (and others) with great compassion.

1 *Karma is not an inevitable, inescapable and dire happening...*
Esoteric Healing Alice A. Bailey (p.296)

Day 22 - Balance

Balance stillness with activity. Recognise what your body needs; by ignoring the call to rest or to take nourishment it suffers and strains.
More difficult for you is the stilling of a mind, tireless in its desire to create.
Know when to pause.
Obey the natural Law: just as the in-breath follows the out-breath, creation is followed by rest.

Your Morning Resolve
Today's very gentle Message speaks for itself. Retreat is a time of rest, even when you are busy. Rest is an attitude - therefore learn to *rest while you are working.*

Recognise when you feel tired or hungry; pause and take a small break. At mealtimes, give yourself adequate time to enjoy and digest your food. Savour each mouthful and its nourishment will magnify.

Aside from your Morning and Evening Practice, take time during the day for absolute stillness.

Breathe ... and *know* you are breathing. Conscious breathing:

- Is an instant way to achieve calm
- Has a powerful effect on the body/mind
- Slows heart rate/normalises blood pressure/eases tension/allows life-force (prana or chi/ki) to flow through the system. *For breath is life, and if you breathe well you will live long on earth* (Sanskrit Proverb)
- Is a meditation in its own right: it can bring us into contact with our Inner Life or Soul

Say to yourself, as you breathe:
I breathe when I feel I'm about to fall (I let my breath rise and I let it fall too).
I breathe when panic rises (I let my breath rise too, and I let it fall).
Always, in my breath I am safe.

Receive the healing power of Fire and resolve today to treat yourself with great kindness and understanding

Day 23 - The Great Healer

What we seek to heal today is not the sickness, or some other limiting situation, but your fear of it. It may be that this negative condition brings a priceless gift that at some point you will recognise as patience, empathy, or wisdom. It may indeed be the *burning ground* of old karma, conditions that once gone through bring an end to negative causes, having their origins in the past. This is why even death is sometimes called the 'great healer' for death eliminates the cause. But why wait for death to experience yourself and others as souls? *See now with the eye of your soul:* trust in the wisdom, strength and courage that eternally guide you.

Your Morning Resolve

For new and better circumstances there has first to be a clearing away of the old. Here we employ again the purging quality of Fire. This is what is meant by 'the burning ground,' also the subject of tomorrow's Message.

Again, we are advised not to *fear* our challenges but to welcome them, safe in the knowledge that they herald beneficent change.

Karma, the Law of Cause and Effect, brings life into perfect balance (cf. the Scales of Justice).

An Exercise in Healing Presence (1)

Selfless service is a great antidote to fear and suffering. It also transmutes karma.

I have included here a few very simple ways to serve, the first for your own healing (see below) and the remaining three for healing others **(see Message 25: My Blessing - Healing Presence (2); Message 28: Kindness – Healing Prayer; and Message 40: Does Your Light Shine? - Healing Circle)**

Self-healing

In order to be of useful service we must attend to ourselves. Firstly then, become a Healing Presence for yourself. For this you need to be firmly anchored in the present moment, without any distractions. How present are you now?

Give great attention to yourself. Feel gratitude, if you can, for your unique and precious life, regardless of your current circumstances, or state of health or mind. Then,

- Attune to your own understanding of Healing Power – a force greater than yourself; the highest you can imagine.
- Recognise your own sacred nature which, despite any human difficulties you may now have, is untouched by them and therefore in perfect 'health.'
- Ask yourself what it is you would like to be healed. At the same time, be open to anything you may as yet be unaware of – e.g. some metaphysical cause of dis-ease that needs to be healed.
- Ask your Highest Imaginable Source of Power to heal you. At the same time give thanks for the healing that is already taking place on your behalf. (Remember, your intentions are already known, your petition acknowledged, your difficulties understood.)
- Do nothing. Simply rest, with open hands, open mind and open heart ... and receive. See only perfection and know that your healing will continue for as long as is needed.
- Finally, acknowledge and humbly give thanks to the Source of Power responsible for the healing.

Day 24 - The Burning Ground

Reflect in the secret place in your heart: how would you live your New Life? What would you transform? Shyness, anxiety, guilt - or something you would rather conceal: a tendency to criticise, to be arrogant, envious, selfish or ambitious? And even more perhaps that you might fail to see outside that secret place in your heart.
What holds you back from living your New Life? And what are you willing to commit to the fire?

Your Morning Resolve
This Message concludes the cycle of Healing and Transformation though both healing and transformation continue unceasingly throughout our lives. Today, we are called to harness the destructive and reshaping power of Fire.

Awareness teaches us to observe ourselves *honestly*, without flinching. Compassion makes this otherwise difficult task bearable. No one is asking you to confess publicly your glamours and foibles. The list will likely be much the same for us all. All you need do is *notice* and *accept.* And, having noticed and accepted, resolve to transform those negative traits into their positive counterparts **(see also Chapter Four: Ray Types, Virtues and Vices).**

Today then, resolve to focus on any long-held beliefs and 'died in the wool' habits. Attitudes that create unrest in your heart: a lack of confidence; jealousy; guilt; irritation, impatience, pride; a tendency to criticise or overly worry.

The very *noticing* of these traits, combined with a good measure of acceptance, compassion, and humour, assists change.
Your intention to enter the Burning Ground and submit these to Fire is all that is required. Already your freedom is assured! You are already creating conditions for a New Life.

The Law of Rebirth ensures that our soul continues its evolution throughout countless lifetimes, learning by its 'failures' through the various Laws of Life, notably Karma. The human soul gathers much experience through its many trials and limitations – the 'schoolhouse of existence.' These trials are important to us – they may be physical hardships, or emotional, mental or spiritual difficulties. Or sometimes all of these. Meanwhile, our ability to endure and overcome ensures our growth (evolution), until eventually (in some lifetime or another), we wake up to the reality of our Inner Life, the soul. At this point we *see* that life is an illusion, masquerading as truth.

The Temple of the Soul is built out of each lifetime's experience. We are building it now, moment to moment. This then is the New Life. A life where only 'the good, the beautiful and the true' remains. Just imagine the experience you have had throughout those countless lifetimes and, setting aside all negatives, see the complex and colourful form that is the result. This is you, not the worldly you with your fears and complexes, but the Inner You; the *real* human being that shines through a little more with each day that passes.

Such a blessing you are to the world!

Chapter Six
Blessing

Rest and receive My Blessing.
And may your body, mind and spirit be filled with the Light of the One Life from which you come and in Whose Be-ing you are eternally present

Blessing[1] is an act of Love; something we are all worthy to receive since it embraces all living beings impartially. It is a gift to be received humbly and open-heartedly.

Blessing embodies the quality of compassion ('feeling with') and the desire to relieve suffering in others. Indeed, the act of blessing inevitably alleviates our own. Blessing is its own reward and invites nothing in return, not even appreciation.

To offer a blessing is not necessarily religious. It arises in response to a desire for wellbeing, gratitude, healing, comfort, and so on, for oneself or another person.

Blessing also signals approval and agreement ('I give it my blessing') – it lends acceptance and encouragement.

To receive a blessing can challenge everything we know, or think we know, and cause us to see life quite differently. They often come out-of-the blue, as signs, miracles or even obstacles. Sometimes we only discover later that a difficulty has actually been a blessing in disguise!
Look back on your life and think of something you have survived (an operation, bankruptcy, a break-up of a relationship, a loss of any kind). Remember a time when your life caved in, as perhaps it has now. If you had been told of this earlier, would you have imagined that you could cope as you have done? Looking back on your life, do you ever think: How on earth did I have the strength to come through all that?

What was the gift your hardship brought you? Has it made you appreciate life more? To be blessed, even in small ways, can often inspire such a beautiful sense of gratitude: a deep bow, a 'thank you' for Life itself.

Or are you still stuck in your hardship, unable to move on? If so, the Messages that follow may help.

My own life has been touched by many such blessings, and many so-called miracles, as I'm sure yours has too:

I have been blessed with an upbringing that allowed me to develop self-reliance, to travel alone through France and Germany at an early age, and to meet my first spiritual guide at nineteen.

Though I disliked school intensely, I was privileged to receive an education that gave me a love of learning and the relentless desire to create.

'Chance meetings' have illuminated my journey of self-awareness, provided insights, broken me apart, shown me facets of myself I would rather disown, made me laugh to tears, restored faith and self-esteem, and so much more.
An unforgettable 'meeting with a Master' in the early 1980s inspired and affirmed my path of service and spiritual direction.

Though there have been many beginnings and endings - three broken marriages, and subsequent loss of savings and financial security - I have been, and still am, always blessed with Love.

Perhaps the most rewarding blessing was the unexpected gift of a son, comparatively late in life at the age of forty-one; one I never cease to give thanks for.

I hope that the eight messages that follow will bless you with health, confidence, love, reassurance, insight, courage, purpose, and whatever else you most need. They will undoubtedly touch each one of us in a unique way.

And finally ...

May you have enough Happiness to fill you up with a caring heart
Enough Trials to give you strength and understanding
Enough Sorrow to keep you human
And enough Hope to bring in each New Dawn

(Source unknown)

1 A glance at the origin of the word reveals more of its meaning. Blessing is derived from Old English *blēdsian, blētsian, bloedsian* - to consecrate with blood, to give thanks, or make holy. Eventually *bloedsian* took on the meaning 'make happy' because of its resemblance to *bliðs* (bliss, grace, or favour). This latter meaning corresponds to our understanding of Blessing as a Divine gift or favour.

Day 25 - My Blessing

Your difficulties are known and understood. That you are dealing with them well has not been overlooked. Continue to be a positive force for those around you for their need is great.
As you stand before Me, rest and receive My Blessing.
And may your body, mind and spirit be filled with the Light of the One Life from Which you come and in Whose Be-ing you are eternally present

Your Morning Resolve

This is one of my favourite messages. It reminds us that we do not go unseen; nor do our challenges and struggles. Congratulate yourself; your courage is rewarded. Know that your fortitude is an inspiration to others. Rest deeply today, even as you attend to your daily tasks. And in resting, receive this Blessing of Light. Take time. Allow it to penetrate your mind, body and spirit. Then open your heart to the healing, comforting nature of Fire. This will encourage you to be a Light for others.
Today, use the Healing Power of Blessing (bless your own life and as many others as you can).

An Exercise in Healing Presence (2)
Healing Presence is a blessing. You can practise it at any time. It can be offered equally at a distance, as in 'distant healing.' Your healing intention will always be registered, if only subconsciously, by others. Remember above all that you are not 'performing healing' on anyone. Healing is a partnership – between you and the Divine, and between you and the person receiving it.

- As before, firstly check that you are fully 'present' in the here and now.
- Attune to your own understanding of an ultimate Healing Power – a force greater than yourself; the highest you can imagine.
- Recognise your own sacred nature which, despite any human difficulties you are experiencing, is untouched by them and is perfect.
- Attune to those you seek healing for. See the sacred in them too. See only their perfection.
- View each one as just 'another you.' Allow a feeling of unity to build silently between you.
- Silently observe without any judgment. Distress or illness may be evident but we do

not necessarily know its cause - or precisely what needs to be healed.

- Ask your Highest Imaginable Source of Power to heal them, each individual in turn. At the same time give thanks for the healing that is already taking place on your behalf. (Remember, your intentions are already known, your petition acknowledged, your difficulties understood.)
- Again, do nothing. Never *try* to heal. Offer it up to the Highest Source of Healing you can imagine. Simply TRUST, and become a clear channel for whatever is needed.
- You will know intuitively how long to remain in Healing Presence. Understand that healing will continue for as long as required.
- Finally, and with humility, give thanks to the Source of Healing.

Resolve today to make Healing Presence a way of life.

At its simplest it is an expression of love and compassion - for oneself and others in equal measure. Our desire to relieve suffering is a testimony to our shared humanity and our fundamental connection with a power greater than ourselves. This is how life appears when we see with the eye of the soul.

Day 26 - Freedom

May freedom be your watchword this day. I am with you as you travel. So, be My Feet, My Hands, My Voice. Be all to Me, unstinting in your love of Life.

Your Morning Resolve

Here once again, a reminder that we are never overlooked, never alone. Whatever our circumstances we are blessed with the ability to bless others. Wherever you go, take inspiration with you. Become that vital link between the Divine and the mundane. Bring all that you gain from your quiet moments into the world. Let all you touch and all you say be expressions of peace, and Fiery Love.

Today, be on fire with your love of life!

Day 27 - The Indwelling God

Who do you think you are? Just a mortal caught up in repeated cycles of pain and pleasure - is this *who* you are? Or, at the heart of your be-ing, do you catch a glimpse that you might be more than this? Place a hand on your chest now. In *here* is who you are ... the *Indwelling God*, the Source of all true security. Remind yourself that no-one and nothing can destroy what you have in here.

Your Morning Resolve

Maybe you feel the victim of your circumstances, afraid of the future, and bereft of hope.

Today, draw on the illuminating power of Fire. Look deeply into yourself and sit once more in Healing Presence. See past your own difficulties, past your current circumstances if you can for a moment. This is your Blessing – the assurance of your Indwelling Eternal Life; your heart, the source of your Fiery Love. Take comfort from this and lift your hand to your heart whenever you need strength and reassurance. Trust ...

Day 28 - Trust

You find it hard to release those you love from your grasp. Bless them instead. Loosen their chains and *trust in their souls.* Both you and they have survived the dangers that have surrounded them so far. Trust that their choices – even their errors - will lead them eventually to higher ground, just as your own have. Believe that, in the end, the soul has autonomy. They know more than you think and are loved, like you, beyond your comprehension. They, like you, are Warriors. Clothe their spirit with love and acceptance - and love them even more. Now is the time to set them free. Thus you may set yourself free of worry.

Your Morning Resolve

It may be that you have anxieties for others. You may fear for their safety, for the choices they make. Healing Presence reminds us to hand these over to a power greater than ourselves. Trust.

Please resist telling someone you are worried about them. Worry doesn't inspire hope. And, don't tell them they look ill or tired – this will only serve to make them feel worse! Also, avoid the commonly used 'take care of yourself' if you can. It can sound subtly ominous, like a warning, even though that is not what you mean to convey.

Love is honest but never destructive. It builds, restores. So today, call upon the creative power of Fire, and rely instead on prayer; on Blessings. Bless others with your faith in them. Bless them with hope. Trust.

If you are experiencing the loss of a loved one, a precious friend, a beloved family member; be patient in your grief. There is much you can do for them in your prayers, with your Healing Presence, with your Love. These will reach them, without doubt, for they are only a thought away. Their essence is very much alive. There is no death – the Indwelling Life is indestructible. Trust.

And for now, and in the coming time, become a gentle and loving companion to yourself. All is well, wonderfully well.

Faith is the substance of things hoped for and the evidence of things not seen. (Hebrews 11: 1)

Day 29 - I Am That

Speak your need to Me now: your need of guidance, of love, of freedom from pain; your need of healing or forgiveness. What is your need?
Open and receive Me. Ask and it is already given. For you are that Love, that Healing, that Forgiveness; that Divinity you seek.
You are that which you need.
Now say 3 times: *I AM THAT. I AM.*

Your Morning Resolve
Today's Message has the illuminating potential of Fire.
Come home to yourself, and take to heart the meaning behind **Day 2's Message**: that we have everything we need within us. *Until you have knelt at your own altar in stillness and reverence you have not found Me.*

Never hold back. Ask for that which you need; and know it is given. All answers to your prayers lie within you, whether they be for guidance, love, freedom, healing, or forgiveness.
Today, listen for answers: guide yourself gently, intuitively. Love yourself deeply, moment to moment. Patiently soothe your own suffering. Be

a Healing Presence for yourself, a faithful companion. Let compassion take the place of self-blame.

Day 30 - I am at your side

Be your own companion and know that I too am always at your side. Leave yourself not, not for a moment. There approaches a time when your great and smaller selves will blend and become One. Then will your years of aspiration and service be consummated. Then will you stride forth with confidence and joy to meet the demands of your calling. My Blessings I leave you.

Your Morning Resolve

Fire warms and comforts, it lights our path in times of difficulty and doubt. Today's message continues the theme of companionship. Just as your Guides and Angels and Teachers are always close by, so too is your Greater Self; the friend who never leaves your side. This is the very Self, the You, who inspires your highest dreams and intentions. Rest today, and enjoy the many blessings of retreat.

Day 31 - Beyond form

So what of the world behind the form, a world of subtle and beautiful reality? This too you know exists. May it be observed? Not only may it be observed but its very existence reveals two truths which, as yet, humanity has failed to grasp:
That all life is interwoven.
That death does not exist.
You are called therefore to *see* these truths, to penetrate matter and to enter the realms of the timeless and formless.
Look on all life with detachment and compassion and you will see. Your clear viewing (*clairvoyance*) allows all that is untrue to fall away. Open your heart and let Life reveal itself to you.

Your Morning Resolve
If only we could see the Life that exists beyond – and even before - the emergence of form itself. That life is the reality; form a pale reflection. Once again, Fire clarifies our vision and illuminates our way.

Today open your heart to the sacred Life within you - a Centre of Consciousness. Mentally bow to the sacred within you and those you meet.

(Again, this is the meaning of that much used phrase *Namaste*: *I bow to the divine in you.*)

Within every form, physical or subtle, is Life. Everything in the manifested world is alive, even space is alive.
Go into Nature or watch from your window and 'notice.' Bow to the Divine Life that ensouls the trees, the earth itself. Develop a relationship with them – a flower or a leaf, a tree. Though the form may change, age and die, the Life within is ageless and undying.

Perhaps the greatest of blessings is the promise of our Immortality.
Another is our interconnection – the magical reality that, even as I write to you now, as you read my words, we are connected – though we may never have met.

Open each day to the miraculous; to new adventures and explorations, if not externally then certainly in your own inner world...

And as you reflect on your own extraordinary life, consider these words:

I am an ordinary person who has been blessed with extraordinary opportunities and experiences. Today is one of those experiences.
Sonia Sotomayor (American Judge)

Day 32 - Be in Love

Go forward now! Apathy and doubt, both born of fear, slow down your steps to freedom.
Be in Love, as Love is within you.
And may your body, mind and spirit be filled with the Light of the One Life from Which you come and in Whose Be-ing you are eternally present.

Your Morning Resolve
To bless is to love deeply, so be in Love and accept everything – even your fears, your doubts...
Love attaches itself to nothing and to no one. It flows freely throughout all creation. So, as you bless, as you love, that blessing flows through you too.
I=LOVE=YOU

Fiery Love is a Blessing we are born to share.
Silently offer your blessing to others, to all living things, to the Earth herself - *I give myself to you as you give yourself to me* - and receive their blessings to you.

As you begin this new day, rest and receive the Blessing of the Present Moment. There are no moments other than this.

Grounded and present, let your breathing be the most important thing in your life right now:

Now while I am nervous and uncertain about the future; in the dark about what tomorrow may bring. Now, even though I may yearn for yesterday, for happier times; I rest, with empty hands, mind and heart, receiving the Blessing this moment brings.

And even when ultimately a new cycle of good fortune arrives … NOW … I am empty. Ready again to be filled with the Blessing of this moment and with everything I need. This moment and 'I' are one.

Chapter Seven
Fiery Love

From the point of Love within the Heart of God
Let love stream forth into the hearts of men.
May Christ return to Earth[1]

(from The Great Invocation)

I wasn't ill, I wasn't dying (it was in fact a fairly unremarkable time in my life), yet in 1981 I left my body behind and had an experience so extraordinary that the memory of it has never left me.

I awoke one night to find the room flooded with light. Within the light was such an exalted and loving Presence that I instantly fell (metaphorically) to my knees. I wasn't dreaming I assure you; actually I have never been as awake as I was right then.

The Presence spoke, uttered a very simple statement - one whose full significance evaded me for another thirty-four years when I finally discovered its relevance.

Deeply humbled, I was aware only of some unspoken work ahead, a sense of joyful anticipation - and above all, the Presence of Perfect Love. I was to experience this again on two more occasions when the Presence returned to me. The first was a visitation that healed me of fear surrounding my health at that time. The second came as a warning of imminent distress, a dark passage of time to follow. Yet even this carried with it the consolation of strength, reassurance, and the certainty of accomplishment.

Apart from anything else these experiences have served as a model for loving, (though one I inevitably fall short of!).

Unconditional love is a global, timeless need. It is the stuff of literature, poems and screenplays, dramas of all kinds. 'Love Conquers All' is a theme that transcends nearly all genres. It tests its characters and is often at the core of their survival, along with themes such as sacrifice, fidelity and betrayal, forgiveness, reconciliation, and triumph over adversity. Unconditional Love, along with unrequited love, frequently dominates the hero's journey. These themes lie deep in our collective experience. Somehow we *know* that True Love is a reality. It is the basis of our nature and something we aspire to despite our limitations.

Love has the capacity to heal anything – even relationships we believe to be irreparably damaged; even too, as I have discovered, when someone has passed on and there is unfinished business to attend to. Past hurts can **always** be healed; all it takes is a little humility, an open heart and a good measure of 'condition-less' love. The beauty is that in giving love in this way we experience it ourselves.

We do not earn love - neither because of nor despite our circumstances. Love is already our right, simply by our being alive.

There is within us all a great Being of Light, whose nature is Fiery Love. Your moments of silence allow you to sense its Presence more clearly. This Being is the greater part of you; your Inner Companion. Meeting your Inner Companion begins with your decision to pause, to turn within. Doing this each day - moment to moment - will change the way to think about yourself, the way you look at life; the way you love.

What do you think might happen if you and I began and ended each day with a focussed thought of Love? This might take the form of a little prayer; a word of comfort for yourself, a nod of understanding. It might be an acknowledgment of your own difficulties and how well you are dealing with them; a blessing, a smile of gratitude for your life. Simply 'thinking Love' is an act of self-compassion. This is, after all, what our retreat is all about.

And what if we taught this simple practice of love and self-caring to our children and grandchildren, offered it to our family and friends, and especially to anyone who is suffering?

Imagine too what *could* happen if one day every member of our human family learned to love himself, herself deeply...
With an unshakeable foundation of self-love we act as living examples of Love. Such is the nature of Fiery Love. **(See Message 33)**.

The Wordless Way, *Awareness*, *Healing and Transformation*, and *Blessing* have all increased our capacity for self-compassion. Let us then begin this final week of retreat with a resolve to love ourselves and others more deeply – even against all odds.

1 *The Great Invocation* is a world prayer. It is an instrument of power to aid the Plan of God find full expression on Earth. www.lucistrust.org

Day 33 - Love against all odds

You are being called to love against all odds, regardless of your circumstances, regardless of how others may treat you. That is the nature of Love, Fiery Love. That is not to say you should allow yourself to be abused. Surely not, for if you do so you collude in the karmic consequences awaiting your abuser.
Once you understand the Laws of Life you will accept responsibility for your every action (or lack of action) and know that whatever you do to another, you do to yourself.

Your Morning Resolve
Perhaps the most significant and illuminating of all the Messages, this one reminds us that our Companion, the Inner Me, knows only love. Its love burns consistently.
But first we need to understand what love is – and what it isn't. Fiery Love must never be confused with the fire associated with sensual love, a fire that burns out of control when it is not requited.
Like the sun, Love shines unfailingly for its own sake and expects nothing in return. Love has no needs.

If you are uncertain how to act in a difficult situation, pause and ask yourself: *What would love do in this case?*
Essentially the answer lies in the tiny space between *reacting* and *responding.* A reaction is usually charged with emotion. At such times we set up an automatic resistance to the situation or challenge. Our heart closes, if only a little.

A response however is more considered; detached, more open to solutions. Responding *keeps your heart open* yet allows you to act assertively, respecting yourself enough to say 'NO!' if necessary. Responding also gives you time to gain a better understanding of the situation or the person causing you difficulties. Trying to 'walk in another's shoes' is a vital step in resolving conflict.

Responding allows you to take the long view and turn away if necessary, leaving time and fate to sort things out.

Today, ask yourself: *What would love do?* Relax, keep your heart open, and draw on the illuminating and creative power of Fiery Love.

Day 34 - We are one

Love, expressed as compassion, flowers from your own struggling and consequent 'reconciliation of opposites' within your own nature: your 'good and bad', your love and hatred, generosity and selfishness, suffering and joy: all will be reconciled some day. Love is when you feel another's pain and want to help, because Love says 'we are one.'

Your Morning Resolve

Compassion grows out of a deep understanding of our own nature. Never forget that Love is the greater part of you and is all-embracing. If you have difficulty in accepting or 'forgiving' some aspect of yourself that you least like, try to understand the hurt or fear or frustration that created it. Every duality is reconciled[1] in Love.

This Message reminds us again of our capacity to love. Love grows as we too grow, aided by the Light of Awareness. Today, draw close to the Fire of your Inner Companion and become a Healing Presence for yourself and for others. **(See also Days 23 and 25).**

1 from the Latin *re-* and *conciliare* (to bring back together)

Day 35 - Generosity

Practise whatever is most difficult for you to do today. That which costs you something and reveals a generosity of spirit – forgiveness; or time for someone in need; or the sharing of something you feel ownership of.
Remove yourself from the Centre Stage where you so love to be. Be silent when you most long to be heard yet speak when you dare not!

Your Morning Resolve
Generosity is inseparable from Love. The purging quality of Fire helps us to go beyond our selfish desires to embrace something larger: a concern for others.

Whenever we 'give away' something we are deeply attached to, it is actually a gift to ourselves. **(See Day 38)**
Giving and receiving are one action.

Forgiveness – the 'giving away' of bitterness, blame, and resentment - is as deeply healing for ourselves as for others; as is self-forgiveness (the 'giving away' of guilt).

To sacrifice[1] is never quite what we think. *True* sacrifice is made spontaneously and readily because for the one who makes it there is no other choice. A higher alternative has already been found so, actually, it costs nothing. Until then it is useful to practice little 'sacrifices', often because this shows us what we are most attached to. Today, ask yourself again: *What would love do?*

- Would love spare a little time for someone in need?
- Would love share freely some original idea of which you are proud and wish to take credit for; one that might serve someone else?
- Would love be as happy to be silent as to be heard?

1 from the Latin: *sacer* (sacred) and *facere* (to make sacred).

Day 36 - Lightness and Peace

I ask you to pause and consider who you are. Despite your current circumstances, go beyond them. Go beyond your feelings, your assumptions, and even beyond your hopes. Let emotion and memory fall away. Stand naked. This act of disrobing brings lightness and peace. There is no-thing more powerful than *you*. So, be who you are: *a point of light and peace in the world.*

Your Morning Resolve

How can we ever alleviate suffering when pain is part of our human condition? Well, we can only do so by identifying, moment to moment, with the Great Being of Light within us. When we do this, when we really do live from the inside out, we find we are so immersed in Love (or joy, or bliss, or anything else we care to call it) that all else fades out of focus. This is the illuminating power of Fire.

Try looking around you now for a few moments. Quietly observe without allowing any thoughts or judgments to enter your mind. When you soften your gaze and look deeply, awareness looks out through your eyes – this is exactly the same awareness as mine (though from a different point of access). You exist; I exist. But you are not a separate self, and neither am I. Together we exist. Your feeling of existing isn't separate from mine. The feeling of existing comes from an undivided 'Whole' and is not separate from what we perceive around us.

There is *no-thing* more powerful than you in this moment. Practise this softening and observing often throughout the day and notice how everything else fades out of focus.
When you are stripped of thoughts, preoccupations, even feelings for a while, only awareness remains; a steady Light. Peace.

Day 37 - Make Peace

Miss no opportunity to make peace. Let there be no temptation to attack, neither to defend. Put aside your need to be right. Be detached, yet with a heart wide open.

Your Morning Resolve

Peace is more than a passive state of serenity. It is an active force. Today we will find many opportunities to 'make' peace, if only with ourselves.

This message reminds us of the creative force released in Fire. It is another call for humility and above all, an open heart. So stay watchful, at a little distance. Soften. Notice the movement of your mind; any flickering of discomfort, irritation, impatience, and so on. Hold your Peace.

Day 38 - Kindness

Kindness, generosity and compassion are never 'given away.' They remain with you. Beneficent thoughts, loving words and unselfish actions all combine to keep you healthy and happy, and remind you that we are indeed one another.

I will never say anything that couldn't stand as the last thing I ever say
Benjamin Zander[1]

Your Morning Resolve

Since our thoughts and words and actions are our own creations, we can never part with them. Energy follows thought, as we know, and always returns to us in one form or another. We make memories for others as well as for ourselves. Therefore we have personal responsibility for each one – and always have moment to moment choices. Whatever you do to others you ultimately do to yourself. This great Truth underlies the whole of creation and is the evidence of our Oneness.

Whatever our thoughts, it is always our intention that counts. Good intentions heal us and others.

When we *choose* to act from our Greater Self we can be certain that no harm is done, to ourselves or others. *What would love do?*

The following simple exercise demonstrates the Healing Nature of Fire. Practised daily it is a gift to us all. It lifts the spirits and has remarkably positive effects on our own wellbeing, as well as on those we seek to help.

An Exercise in Healing Prayer

- Firstly, have a notebook dedicated to healing prayers, a place to enter the names of those who have requested help.
- It is 'healing etiquette' to receive permission from those who require healing. When this is not possible I make a petition to the individual's Inner Self and proceed in a 'Thy Will Be Done' fashion. Healing Prayer is an offering from one soul to another, the healer being the instrument for the highest available source of healing power.
- Healing into Dying is a very privileged form of service. Our prayers are always beneficial both during the dying process and after transition.

- Evening is a good time to practise this form of healing. It encourages deep relaxation and restful sleep to follow.
- Make a conscious connection with the highest source of healing you can envision – an angel, guide or some spiritual being that you relate strongly to.
- Ask that each person on your list, yourself included, may receive the healing that they need, in mind, body and spirit. You may find that your hands begin to tingle or grow warm just as though the person were physically present. I then hold my hand/s over each name in turn and quietly say a few words of healing, whatever comes to mind in the moment.
- If you have a very long list to go through and little time available you may ask that everyone on the list receive healing. (I personally prefer to speak each name aloud but you may not find this necessary.
- It can be useful to make a few notes during or after the Healing session. Any recorded information can be useful to the individuals prayed for and allows them to play an active part in the healing process.

- At the end of your Healing session always remember to ask for healing for yourself. Always close with thanks to those healing guide/s who have overseen the session.

1 Benjamin Zander, conductor of the Boston Philharmonic Orchestra and co-author of *The Art of Possibility – practices in Leadership, Relationship and Passion*

Day 39 - Fiery Love

Many believe that the world as we know it will come to an end. Indeed it must, for Fiery Love cannot tolerate injustice. These are the 'end times' indeed, an end to greed and separation, an end eventually to poverty and war, born of injustice. Something big is about to happen. A great Light has already come into the world, the Embodiment of Love. We are about to witness a transformation like none other before it.

Your Morning Resolve

It's easy to get so caught up in our personal misfortune that we forget the global difficulties of which we are a part. Human greed, self-forgetting, and the illusion of separateness on a mass scale, have led us many times to the brink of destruction. We are now at that point once more. Poised between catastrophe (the consequence of illusion and separation) and redemption (the acceptance of Oneness and Brotherhood), the future of humanity is in the balance.

Something big is about to happen - war, injustice, extremes of poverty and wealth, can no longer be sustained on Earth since these violate every Law of Life. Destruction of the old must inevitably precede creation of the new.

And herein lies hope for our future - a New Light has come into the World. Do you sense it?
Our active participation is called for. Now more than ever, each one of us has the task of creating a New World. This is not airy idealism; it is common sense. We are the World Savers.

What then can we do?

1. In a very practical way we can give our support to those groups of 'world changers' who call for justice through petitioning and peaceful demonstrations.

2. We can devote our retreat time *right now* to strengthening our spiritual connections – with ourselves and with others.

3. We can pray sincerely for all who work towards the betterment of life on Earth.

4. We can pray also for those (especially those in positions of power) who are un-awakened, and unresponsive to their own Inner Life.

In each of these ways we draw on the creative and healing forces of Fire.

Day 40 - Does your light shine?

How brightly does your fire burn?
Notice what happens when you put your own needs to one side and attend to the suffering of others. Your own suffering is lifted. You begin to feel lighter …
You SHINE!
See what happens when you put aside your need to be right, when you make peace. When you have no further need to attack or defend … No need even for words.
You SHINE!
So SHINE, as only you can shine. You touch many, many hearts with your Fiery Love.

Your Morning Resolve
This final stage of our journey is demanding nothing less than your full identification with the Being of Light that lives within you **(cf. Day 36).** This is what it means to be one of the World Savers, the World Changers; the Peacemakers. Regardless of your circumstances – maybe even because of them – you are more than equipped. Don't ever underestimate the part you play!

In *Fiery Love* we have explored the 'downward path' to self-understanding. We have found that *it is precisely through our daily tests and trials that we grow in self-awareness and understanding. Yes, it's right down here in the thick of things that we ultimately transcend our difficulties.*

Whenever we go within, even for a few minutes each day, we will open up to powers beyond our imagination. Silence is the beginning and the end.

In Silence we become - literally - a point of Light and Peace in the World. Light and Peace are then no longer symbolic but a reality - you radiate Fiery Love.

Let us imagine that you and I are joining right now with other Points of Light and Peace around the world. In thought and intention we link hearts and create our own Circle of Love, Light and Peace; a Healing Circle.

A Healing Circle

A Healing Circle is similar in practice to Healing Prayer (**Day 38: An Exercise in Healing Prayer**).

Group healing can greatly magnify the effects of prayer. Whether the group is large or small each individual Point of Light and Peace plays his or

her part equally. It is not dependent on its participants being physically present.
There are many stories reported of 'miracles' that have occurred as a result of group prayer and Healing Circles.
As in Healing Prayer (Distant Healing) every healing petition and intention crosses apparent barriers of time and space. For the Inner Life, or Soul, there is no 'there,' only HERE; no 'then' or 'when,' only NOW.
You touch many hearts with your Fiery Love.

This beautiful act of service benefits the one who prays as much as those prayed for; as we touch hearts we find that our own hearts are touched too. With every thought of Love and Light for others we receive more Love and Light ourselves. We shine!

The Best is Yet to Come!

It is here as we complete our retreat that we suddenly find ourselves back on *The Wordless Way*:

In silence you become calm, compassionate and mindful; a transmitter of Fiery Love.

And what better way to end than to begin again? To walk each Fiery Pathway afresh with renewed understanding. When you do you will find that each Message yields something new, just as you and I are made new with each passing day.

Do you remember the notes you made on the eve of your retreat? Have a look at them now. Remind yourself why you decided to enter retreat and what you hoped to gain from it.

Take time to reflect and ask yourself the following:

1. Have your hopes been fulfilled – at least some of them?
2. What especially have you discovered about yourself during this time?
3. How has your experience of Silence changed you?

4. Are you now inclined to rest more, even when you are working?
5. Are you more self-aware, more mindful of your thoughts, feelings, and what drives you?
6. Are you now able to grace yourself with love and compassion? To feel so worthy of love and compassion that you are able to share them freely with others?
7. Do you now know beyond all doubt that YOU alone create your life and how you live it, regardless of your circumstances?

If you can answer just one of these positively your time has not been wasted!

This is your precious Life Story and it's far from over. The best is yet to come. Challenges and opportunities will arise from time to time: and new characters will appear, as in any good story. They are all there for a purpose, and though their meaning may not always be discerned till much later – just make the most of each one.

Finally, with each passing moment never once forget the author of your Life: the great Being of Light within you, the 'you' at your Centre.

Though your circumstances may change (for all things pass) so too will you, as well as the way you deal with them.
And one thing is certain: the 'you' at your Centre will guide you safely through them all.

May you be well, may you be happy, may you be free from suffering ...

Appendix

Fiery Love in Action
Creating a Heart Centre in your Local Community:

The Centre for Spiritual Growth and Healing

Moyra Irving is co-founder of *The Centre for Spiritual Growth and Healing* **(CSGH)**, currently based at the Quaker Meeting House in Newcastle-under-Lyme, Staffordshire. The **CSGH** is a group initiative, launched in 2004, to promote spiritual development, healing partnerships, and a climate of hope and inspiration in a fearful world. It is completely non-sectarian and you are welcome to visit us whether or not you have any particular religious or spiritual faith.
The Centre operates on a monthly basis and is run totally by volunteers, and funded by kind donations from visitors.

It may be that you wish to set up a similar project in your own area. Please do get in

touch – Moyra will be happy to answer your questions.[1]

The idea was born during a time of personal challenge and for Moyra proved to be something of a life saver. The opportunity to be of service to others is deeply gratifying. It can also be a powerful antidote to depression and loneliness, and often restores a sense of purpose, which is healing in itself.

What we can offer you:

At the Centre we offer workshops on meditation, spiritual growth and complementary healing. Many of our visitors come to meet people of like mind. Nearly all comment on the loving atmosphere created at the **CSGH**, and have come to experience it as a 'heart centre' within the local community.

Many already find complementary healing extremely beneficial but are unable to meet the cost of regular visits to therapists. This is where our **Free Healing Clinic** can help. The Clinic is staffed by professional healers and holistic therapists who offer their time and skills free of charge.

Free Healing Clinic:

We offer a variety of therapies including Spiritual Healing, Reconnective Healing, No-Hands Massage, Reiki, Angelic Reiki, Eternal Light Healing, Reflexology, Aura Some Colour Therapy, Indian Head Massage, and more. We also have guest speakers, experts in their own field, who offer presentations on specific therapies or healing techniques.

Appointments for therapies and talks are made on arrival. All events are free of charge and include refreshments and car parking (at the rear of the building). However, since we are not funded by any outside agency, donations are gratefully accepted as these help us to continue our work.

Your comments are always valuable to us and help us to improve our service and meet your personal needs. Our Reception staff or any of our volunteers are happy to answer your questions.

Clinic shop:

While you are waiting for your appointment you can purchase good quality second hand books and relaxation / meditation / spiritual growth videos, DVDs and CDs in our Clinic Shop You can also help yourself to a variety of free magazines and information leaflets about forthcoming events, or simply relax with a cuppa from our pop-up café and meet new friends. Proceeds from sales go to *The Extra Guest* charity, funding end-hunger projects around the world: www.theextraguest.com

Healing Circle:

At the close of each clinic we invite you to join our Healing Circle. This involves a powerful guided meditation – an opportunity for you to request healing for yourself and for others. No previous experience is needed and all are welcome.

Events (Times and Dates):

(1) Meditation, Healing and Spiritual Growth workshops (2.00 – 4.30 pm)

These are held on the 1st Saturday of March, June, September and December (*A Festival of Light*).

(2) Clinics are held on the 1st Saturday of January/February/April/May/July/August/ October and November. Doors open at 1.20 pm. Prompt arrival is essential in order to secure an

appointment. The Healing Circle begins after the last appointment (approximately 4.40 pm.)

Would you like to help?

If you are a professionally trained and insured healer or therapist (or if you are a student healer/therapist insured by your teacher or training body) and would like to offer your time and skills to the Healing Clinic, we would love to hear from you. The Clinic provides a safe and supportive healing environment as well as an opportunity to work within a committed team. Many healers have said how much their own practice has been enhanced by working as part of this group.

Every volunteer in our practice knows that healing is not just about what we do with our hands. What we say, how we listen, and how we value each visitor adds to their experience and can open them up to a new sense of themselves. Although we can never guarantee a cure perhaps the greatest benefit of our Free Healing Clinic is this:

Increasing numbers of people turn up each month, seeking relief, reassurance, or even a sense of direction. Often they go away with far more than they bargained for, having been awakened at some level or other to a new perception of life.

1 For all enquiries please contact: moyrairving@yahoo.co.uk

Moyra Irving
(Co-founder)

Trisha Tweedie
(CSGH Coordinator)

Marilyn Lockett
(Healers/Therapists Coordinator)

Printed in Great
Britain
by Amazon